RICHARD MEIER

RICHARD MEIER

Claudia Conforti
Marzia Marandola

Richard Meier

Cover
J. Paul Getty Center for the Fine Arts, Los Angeles
Photo
Scott Frances / Esto © The J. Paul Getty Trust

Translation
Soget srl

minimum
essential architecture library

Series edited by Giovanni Leoni

Published Titles

Santiago Calatrava
Pier Luigi Nervi
Álvaro Siza

For the excerpts reproduced in the sections
"Thought" and "Critique," the authors and publishers
wish to thank those who have authorised their
publication. The publisher is available for any queries
regarding sections for which it has not been possible
to trace the holder of the rights.

© 2009 24 ORE Motta Cultura srl, Milan
© 2009 Il Sole 24 ORE Business Media srl, Milan

First edition: March 2009

ISBN: 978-88-6413-004-0

Printed in Italy

Contents

Portfolio

Introduction

Introductory essay written by Claudia Conforti

Meier: between avantgardism and modernity

" …architecture adorns the Universe, makes cities extremely comfortable, protects them from the violence and hidden dangers of enemies, transports the necessary waters, contains them when necessary, and makes them convenient and useful…"

Giovan Battista Armenini, *De' veri precetti della pittura*, Ravenna 1586.

With the New York Five

"New York 1969: at a meeting organised by the Conference of Architects for the Study of Environment (Case Group), at the Museum of Modern Art (MoMA), the English architect Kenneth Frampton presents the work of five New York architects – Peter Eisenman, Michael Graves, John Hejduk, Charles Gwathmey, Richard Meier – whose group recognition was to be sanctioned three years later by the book *Five Architects*, edited by Wittenborn, with foreword by Arthur Drexler, contributions from Colin Rowe, Frampton, William La Riche and the architects themselves[1]." With these words, Manfredo Tafuri (1935-1994) recalled the public debut of the Five and then immediately pointed out the promotional nature of the association between them, united particularly by the refusal of content related and reductive interpretations of the architecture, which dominated at that time.

Collective presentation, which was wanted above all by Eisenman, the theorist of the group, was orchestrated under the critical profile by Frampton himself, and supported by Rowe (1920-1999), ingenious English architect and critic, who was to admit years later that "it was a question of political convenience and controversy[2]." "A temporary life raft[3]" as Tafuri defined it, launched as a way of recognising and creating openings for young architects – all in their thirties and forties – in the harsh world of American professionalism.

The presentation refers to another presentation at the MoMA, organised in 1932 by the critic Henry-Russell Hitchcock (1903-1987) and the architect Philip Johnson (1906-2005)[4]; the exhibition and catalogue, called *The International Style: Architecture since 1922*, cleared the way for modern European architecture in the United States, from Le Corbusier (1887-1965) to Mies van der Rohe (1886-1969), and from Gropius (1883-1969) to Oud (1890-1963). The *Five* operation alludes to that famous precedent, both in terms of the five laying claim to the inheritance of the International Style, and in terms of the hope of repeating the crucial success.
As it was to be.
The presentation was a success. Followed by exhibitions in London (1975) and Naples (1976), it established the five architects from New York in the professional and academic world, not only in America, who then all obtained rather different results after being launched together.
Who was Richard Meier at the time of the *Five*'s debut?
Born in Newark into a Jewish family of German origin, Richard Alan Meier graduated in architecture at Cornell University in 1957. After military service, in 1959, he embarked on a trip around Europe, visiting the birthplaces of modern architecture. The buildings Le Corbsuier built at Weissenhofsiedlung in Stuttgart (1927) struck the young American, who boldly turned up in Paris at the master's studio, offering his services, which were rejected. Fate gave him another chance though; at the inauguration of the Maison du Brésil, designed by Le Corbusier and Lucio Costa (1902-1998), at the Cité Universitaire complex, Meier took advantage of Le Corbusier's presence, getting to him early on for a conversation which, even though finished with another refusal, was to shape the young architect's talent[5]. Indeed Meier was to be charmed for a long time by the unconventional, austere hedonism that marks Corbu's first production, that which Rowe calls "cardboard."
Since the first Le Corbusier, Meier has extracted the essence of those principles, evident in his work-walkways like animated structures in space, formalisation of the structural cage, geometric purism, free forms intersecting and turned into perfect stereometry, the use of white which modulates surfaces and converses with the light, the concise essentiality of exteriors contrasting with complex interior spatial organisation, the modernist

opposite page
High Museum of Art, Atlanta, 1980-1983; nocturnal view of entrace ramp

[1] M. Tafuri, "Les bijoux indiscrets", in *Five Architects NY*, catalogue of the exhibit in Naples, edited by C. Gubitosi and A. Izzo, Rome: Officina Edizioni, 1976, p. 9. The title of the essay is the same as a picture by F. Stella in 1974. The piece is republished in M. Tafuri, "Le ceneri di Jefferson", in *La sfera e il labirinto. Avanguardie e architettura da Piranesi agli anni '70*, Turin: Einaudi,1980, pp. 361-371. The American edition of the catalogue was published in 1975 with a postscript by P. Johnson, underling the importance of history for Richard Meier and wishing the begin of Meier's "not Corbusier" phase.
[2] See interview in R. Einaudi, "L'opera di Richard Meier: origini e influenze" in *Richard Meier e Frank Stella: una conversazione tra architetto e artista*, editing by Peter Slatin and in *Richard Meier Frank Stella*, catalogue of the exhibit in Rome, edited by M. Costanzo, V. Giorgi, M.G. Tolomeo, Milan: Electa, 1993, p. 34.
[3] M.Tafuri, "Les bijoux indiscrets", cit., 1976, p.11.
[4] L. Sacchi, "Richard Meier o la rappresentazione della modernità" in *Richard Meier. Architetture*, by P. Ciorra, Milan: Electa, 1993, pp. 8-9.
[5] Interview at Arte (Association Relative à la Télévision Européenne), 21 June 2008; L. Sacchi, *Richard Meier o la rappresentazione della modernità*, cit., 1993, p.10.

Smith House, Darien, 1965-1967; south view with chimney and external staircase

6 On relationships with Europe see K. Frampton, "Progetti in Europa di Richard Meier & Partners", in *Casabella*, 574, December 1990, pp. 4-20.
7 R. Meier, "Preface" in *Richard Meier Museums 1973-2006*, New York: Rizzoli, 2006, p. 8.

metaphor of the steamboat, the normalising use of details, ranging from fixtures to the tubular, mesh railings, taken from seamanship. Above all, however, similarly to the French-Swiss master, Meier also arranges and designs perspective progressions to the millimetre, which have to guide the perception of each of his architectural structures. From the scale of the landscape to closer use, to the interior reconnaissance, every spatial thoroughfare connected to his constructions is carefully calibrated in a visual function and nothing is left to chance. This ingenuous, perceptive obsession pushes Meier to meticulously check photographs (and the interpreting photographers) that depict his work and suggest the unfailing "night effects", which furnish his publications and transform his architecture into magic lanterns which float in nature.

By exhibiting a scale model of the Savoye Villa (1928-31) on his office, Meier acknowledges, with cunning self-assurance, his debt to Le Corbusier. Yet Meier houses are extremely different from Corbu prototypes, first of all with respect to the dimensions, which are incomparably larger in Meier's work. The construction techniques are also different. In Corbu's work, reinforced concrete, brick and plaster turn the *pondus* and *gravitas* into sublime abstraction while in Meier, self-supporting wooden panels, very slim cylindrical pillars in steel and glass membranes tilt

the kaleidoscope of light and transparency. Moreover, on an expressive level, Meier's building structures, cracked by bottomless voids, detract from the frontal perspective and hierarchy of the views, to the advantage of a rounded sculptural superiority. The frontal architecture is an ambiguous achievement of the maturity of Meier, as shown by his Neugebauer house (1995-1998) which, built along a linear axis, demonstrates two façades of frontal perfection, and before that by the very elegant Rachofsky House (1991-1996) in Dallas. Previously, the double façade was tried in Barcelona's Museum of Contemporary Art (1987-1993), followed by the Ara Pacis Museum in Rome (1995-2006); two examples where the frontal perspective and hierarchical graduality of the façades are conditioned by the intense urban nature of the setting.

Europe & America

On a methodological (and formal) front, Meier's debts are multiple and varied; from Walter Gropius to Louis Kahn (1901-1974), Frank Lloyd Wright (1867-1959) to Alvar Aalto (1898-1976) and Marcel Breuer (1902-1981), not to mention Francesco Borromini (1599-1667) and Johann Balthasar Neumann (1687-1753), masters of that over-elaboration of light that Meier admires so unreservedly that in 1973, as resident architect at the American Academy in Rome, he took his students to Bavaria to visit the Baroque sanctuaries instead of the classical Mediterranean locations, as was the custom[6].

The two shores of the Atlantic meet in Meier's architecture, who states: "I have worked with the European and American tradition of spatial expression […] and what interests me is a synthesis of the two[7]."

A syncretic attitude worthy of Meier, who is unique among American architects and an extraordinary European success, attested to by dozens of examples of his work spread around the old continent.

Ever since the initial houses, Meier (1963-1965), Smith (1965-1967), Hoffman (1966-1967) and Saltzman (1967-1970), Meier has overthrown architecture's internal space in nature, transplanting the vigorous nostalgia of the origins of American tradition – superbly interpreted by Wright – into the European legacy. Engulfing nature in architecture's soul, the architect revives the "electrifying" effect, which he experienced from *Falling Water*, especially

"the extension of internal space in the landscape, or rather, the visual extension of Falling Water in the surrounding environment[8]."
If the visual reciprocal penetration between the interior and nature finds its origin in Wright, in the Prairie Houses and especially in Falling Water, the house on the waterfall (1934-1937), there is no shortage of American examples, which are less famous internationally but that nevertheless know how to deviate between artificiality and nature and between architecture and landscape with lyrical vigour. Of particular importance among these, and not by chance, is the house built in Des Moines between 1936 and 1937 by George Kraetsch for Earl Butler, appropriately highlighted by Livio Sacchi as "prophetic, symbolic anticipation" of the opulent extension of the Art Center, which Meier completed between 1982 and 1984 in Des Moines[9].
Autonomy of architecture and intimate collusion with nature as well as a "relationship between built form and natural topography[10]" are the cornerstones of Meier's thinking, which unfurl a superlative effectiveness in the arts acropolis in the hills of Brentwood, where lies the gigantic art complex among the rough nature of California, built for the Getty Center in Los Angeles (1985-1997). When there is an absence of nature, however, as with the heart of the ancient cities in Europe, these principles

are thrown into crisis and Meier's perfect structures get enmeshed by an insidious self-centredness which detaches them from, and renders them alien to, the artificial and layered setting of the ancient city. Self-sufficient architecture, not necessarily anti-urban but rather a-urban, Meier's buildings allude to suspended, remote harmonies, insensitive to the viscous temporality of the city.
To now, one might anticipate that the passionate objections that opposed, and still oppose, the Museum of Contemporary Art in Barcelona, and the Ara Pacis Museum in Rome, opulent crystal fixtures in the live body of ancient cities, are not alien to the instinctive awareness of that aristocratic detachment that distances Meier's cold propositions from irregular Mediterranean construction.
Upon returning from Europe, Meier embarked on an intense professional apprenticeship in the studios of New York, initially with Davis, Brody and Wisniewski (1959), then with S.O.M from 1959 to 1960, and finally with Marcel Breuer from 1961 to 1963.
The experience, which was undertaken between the professional extremes of Skidmore, Owing and Merrill, noble quintessence of the lucrative American profession, and the craftsman's "workshop" of the Hungarian exile Breuer, demonstrates the double USA/European track upon which Meier's choices ran very well[11].

Saltzman House, East Hampton, 1967-1969; view from the south with guest rooms and aerial corridor

[8] C. Jenks, "Interview with Richard Meier", in *Richard Meier. Buildings and Projects 1979-89*, London: 1990, cited in R. Einaudi, *L'opera di Richard Meier…*, cit., 1993, p. 33.
[9] L. Sacchi, *Richard Meier o la rappresentazione della modernità*, cit., 1993, p. 8.
[10] R. Meier, "Preface", cit., 2006, p. 9.
[11] F. Dal Co, "Lo stile di Meier", preface in K. Frampton, *Richard Meier*, Milan: Electa, 2003, p. 7; it underlines the centrality of his experience with Breuer.

Contemporary Art
Museum, MACBA,
Barcelona, 1987-1995;
front entrance facing the
square

The Brush and the Set Square

In 1963 the architect opened a studio in New York
and started with an arrangement at the Jewish
Museum of an exhibition on the architecture of
American synagogues, of which he is creator and
curator. This was the first of a series of
arrangements created by Meier, such as that at the
Design State Museum of Albany for the New York
School exhibition (1977), and then for the
inauguration of the Cooper-Hewitt Museum in New
York (1976). The manager of the Jewish Museum,
Alan Solomon, already Meier's professor and an
influential critic who organised exhibitions on
Jasper Jones and Robert Rauschenberg, published
the book *New York: The New Art Scene*, with
photographs by Ugo Mulas (1967). With the
exhibition "Recent American Synagogue
Architecture", Meier ideally reintegrated
architecture into artistic experimentation, which
was undergoing an exciting season in New York
during those years.

His peculiar beginning, which blends cultural
promotion and critical action, reveals an unorthodox,
if not shocking attitude, of Meier towards American
professionalism and attests to an eccentric
personality; a voracious, cultured intellectual from the
East Coast, who made good use of the university
teachings of Vladimir Nabokov and John Hartell, and
an architect who is committed to society, working
with the progressive Urban Development
Corporation, drawing up the Bronx urban
development plan in 1969, within which he designed
the council estate Twin Parks Northeast Housing
(1969-1973) and the Development Center
(1970-1977) for psychiatric patients.
Above all else, however, Meier an artist, rapacious
and omnivorous. He studied painting at New School
and furiously practiced it during stolen moments, in
a makeshift workshop in West Broadway, which
was freed up at night by Frank Stella, in a loft
rented with Michael Graves. He burnt out his
experimental frenzy of the Sixties with artists such
as Frank Stella and Barnett Newman (1905-1970),

Ara Pacis Museum, Rome,
1995-2006

the latter exhibiting his model of a synagogue
outlined as a baseball stadium at the Jewish
Museum, with Philip Johnson and Louis Kahn[12].
In Meier's vast, artistic horizon, it is possible to
recognise the European impression of the unity of
the arts, whereas architects ranging from
Michelangelo to Le Corbusier, Meier's chosen
mentors, handle the set square, brush and chisel
without distinction[13]. Even after having opted for the
architectural profession, studying at night in private,
during time stolen from studying architecture, Meier
continued to sculpt and create collages; a training
ground for the hands and eyes, an exercise in
designing museums, spaces of art and for art, which
moved away from his charming fairy-tale residences.
The Meier-styled creativity also found an outlet in
teaching, to which he became devoted at the Cooper
Union, run by Hejduk, from 1963 to 1973. After
1973 and his stay at the American Academy in
Rome, then managed by the eclectic inspiration of
Henry Milon, Meier limited his teaching to short,
enthusiastic spurts at UCLA, Harvard and Yale.

Design Strategies

Like the builders of ancient temples and cathedrals,
Meier studied a very limited type of environment in
depth for years, and this allowed him extraordinary
refinements and results. In the first phase, between
the sixties and the mid-seventies, the house was at
the centre of his designs. The museum defined the
second phase of Meier's architectural work,
which, without a solution of continuity, ensured
the elements of a constituent, expressive abacus
in museums with open-minded genius, which
were perfected in previous study, to such
an extent as to establish a fertile transitivity
between house and museum: the house turns out
to be a small private museum and the museum
a house for collective use.
Since the mid-eighties the work of Meier has been
of two different types. There have been numerous
office buildings: the two Bridgeport Center towers
in Connecticut (1984-1989), the Siemens building
in Munich (1984-1990), the Royal Dutch paper

[12] The episode is
remembered by Meier in
"Richard Meier e Frank
Stella: una conversazione
tra architetto e artista",
in P. Slatin, *Richard Meier
Frank Stella*, cit., 1993,
p. 212.
[13] Conversation with Stella
on Meier's fondness for
Michelangelo is eloquent.
Ivi, pp. 208-209.

25

High Museum of Art,
Atlanta, 1980-1983;
entrance halls with
circular ramps

three tower blocks in Perry and Charles Street (1999-2006), and those for the FSM East River contract, both in New York. Buildings and projects which, as with the towers designed for Wijnhaven Kwartier in Den Haag (2001), attest to impeccable professionalism, which nevertheless do not fully convey the poetic lyricism which renders Meier's houses and museums unmistakeable masterpieces. The repetition of serial elements, which characterise the residential buildings and offices, harnesses the explosive, sculptural inspiration of Meier in conventionally built structures, which manage to express themselves admirably, especially in individual parts. This is demonstrated at Dio Padre Misericordioso Church (1996-2004), built in Rome for the Jubilee in 2000, where the exaggerated reinforced concrete canopies of the chapel and the baptistry draw on the wondrous persuasiveness of the myth[14]. Yet the most seductive results from the Meier studio, split into two locations since 1986, one in New York and the other in Los Angeles, remain those of the original building types; in the house and the museum, the sculptural modelling of space joins with transitive sensuality which knows how to connect architecture to art and nature, by materialising perfect visual machinery. It wasn't by chance that Hejduk, introducing Meier in Florence in 1981, described him as "a man who uses few words but many images[15]." How natural it was for someone like Meier to view architecture as an art, stating that "architecture is an art of substance[16]." Meier is interested in the creation of heavily abstract formal systems, diagrams that layer into a "system of systems" and generate a poetically reactive object, capable of seducing the senses and conversing with the intellect. This method was illustrated in 1974 in *Casabella* 389 by Meier himself, who called the piece *Design Strategies* and included every plan of the related diagrams. The site, the functional and distributive plans, the circulation, the entrances, the structure and the boundaries (or infilled areas), are the diagrammatical constraints which accompany the photographs of the buildings as prologues, and replace the sketches which the architect tends not to divulge. From the morphology of the land, the layout of the trees, the coastline and the panoramas, like a surveyor of ancient times, Meier separates fundamental layouts which order structures, deep voids and curvilinear intrusions, which bring the lesson of Alvar Aalto to life. The geometric origins of the design lies in the site

mills at Hilversum in Holland (1987-1992), Canal+ Headquarters in Paris (1988-1992), Euregio in Basel (1990-1998), and Swissair North America at Melville, New York (1991-1994). There is no shortage of organisational headquarters and public buildings, such as the town hall and the Central Library in Den Haag (Holland 1989-1995), the amazing Sandra Day O'Connor Federal Court at Phoenix in Arizona (1995-2000), Camden Hospital in Singapore (1990-1999), the fantastic roof of the Performing Arts Center designed in 2001 for Bethel in New York. Meier also repeatedly tackles commercial structures, such as the project in Germany for Peek & Cloppenburg, where he built a large warehouse in Dusseldorf (1998-2001, and horizontal and vertical residential complexes. Examples of the first type are the Espace Pitôt at Montpellier in France (1988-1993) and the terraced houses recently completed at Jesolo Lido Village (2003-2008). The second type includes the

[14] A complete study of the church in A. Falzetti, *La chiesa Dio Padre Misericordioso*, Rome: CLEAR, 2003.
[15] J. Hejduk, in *Richard Meier*, catalogue of the exhibit in Florence, edited by G. Pettena, Venice: Marsilio 1981, p. 13.
[16] R. Meier, "Preface", cit., 2006, p. 8.

which, after his long stay in Rome, Meier captures in the orthogonal grids reminiscent of the Roman encampments: double orientation grills which incorporate the land morphology and plot configuration into the geometric pattern. The various geometries collide and overlap each other, generating the spatial directrix of the building; wall coverings in porcelain steel panels and stone plates redesign the same geometric pattern.

The Supremacy of the Gaze

In Meier's houses and museums, one does not enter at ground level; a ramp leaning like the gangway onto a ship, a suspended pathway or a winding staircase, capture the first floor directly, where the spectacular core of the building unfolds to coincide with the communal area, the living room, museum foyer or hallway of a public building. The entrances, which Meier tirelessly deviate from the norm, emphasise the dialogue between structure and landscape, and underline the nature of the sculpted object placed on the land. In Smith House a miniscule ramp connects the rustic border to the first floor and divides the opaque screen of panels in the private rooms; a similar system appears in the charming Shamberg House in Chappaqua and in the Douglas House, where the ramp is replaced with a daring walkway which is even berthed to the terrace; the most panoramic place in the house is similar to a ship's gangplank. In Saltzman House, the entrance on the first floor is by means of a straight bridge that connects the area with the guest rooms to the main block. Similarly in the very elegant Grotta House a horizontal walkway connects the grassy slope to the private opaque front of the residence. A not too dissimilar system was used in the house of Old Westbury, whereas in the house at Winchester the entrance comprises a gradual sequence of ramps and steps laid along the slope, which is thus geometrical. The correspondence between the entrance and the unseen private wing is contradicted in the compact multi-linear installation in Rachofsky House, where the stepped walkway with top bridge is emphasised by the inclusion of a surprising partition, covered in porcelain steel panels. The slanting walkway and the stepped ramp explode in the astonishing monumentality of the entrance of the Atheneum, New Harmony (1975-1979), the explosive masterpiece that inaugurates the artistic maturity of

Meier and moulds the sophisticated elegance of the entrance ramps of the High Museum, Atlanta (1980-1983). The high entrance imposes a temporal, spatial and perceptive graduality on the exterior/interior passage, which gives it a slow, ritualistic effect. For every muscular contraction of the body there is a corresponding elevation in height and a widening of the horizon, and the light plays the main role. Consequently the vertical connections, in the heart of the building, are illuminated from above; the intensity of the light increases step by step with the height and gradual widening of the view.

The changing of the light marks the metaphysics of time and space in Meier's architecture, which is why it suits museums wonderfully; the modern cathedrals of the new, planetary religion of art. Localised and calibrated by Meier according to the views, the entrances and pathways transcend their function. Like the *promenades architecturales* of Le Corbusier they are unique, complex, perceptive tools of experience; movement and gaze unite with the landscape through the architecture. Trees, rocks, fields, reflections from water and the sky, inlay a kaleidoscope of snow-white beauty with roofs, walls, pillars and beams. Anyone who has walked the pulsating ramps in the heart of the Atheneum, the double perimeter ramp of the Museum of Decorative Arts in Frankfurt (1079-1985), the ramp in the Museum of Contemporary Art in Barcelona (1987-1993), or the curved balcony ramps which border the dizzying high frame in the High Museum of Atlanta, cannot forget the almost mythical intensity of the sensory experience.

The functional buildings loom tree-like around the *promenades*, reflected by the structure and the infilled areas; the structure is dot-like, marked by very slim, steel, circular pillars in the communal areas where space flows with the light and should have no obstacles; it is continuous and box-like in the areas kept for individual use, the bedrooms, toilets and guest rooms, and exhibition rooms, reading rooms and offices. Infilled areas are opaque, compact and orthogonal when delimiting private areas, held by continuous, perforated membranes or transparent diaphragms when screening communal spaces.

The supremacy of the gaze that permeates Meier's architecture seems to be represented in the emblem of the great humanist architect Leon Battista Alberti (1404-1472); an eye opened wide to the world, lifted by the wings of fame onto a universe which is posing the question *Quid Tum* (So what?).

Chronology

1934	Born in Newark, New Jersey
1957	Obtained degree from Cornell University, Ithaca, New York, enrolled in 1952
1961	Lambert Beach House, Fire Island, New York
1963	Exhibition of Recent American Synagogue Architecture, Jewish Museum, New York Meier House, Essex Fells, New Jersey (completed in 1965)
1964	Tender for Benjamin Franklin Parkway, Philadelphia, Pennsylvania (with Frank Stella) Dotson House, Ithaca Sona New York Showroom for handicrafts and textiles, New York (with E. Lustig Cohen) Renfield House, Chester, New Jersey (with E. Lustig Cohen; completed in 1966)
1965	Studio house for Frank Stella, New York (completed in 1966) Tender for the Arts Centre of the University of California, Berkeley (with John Hejduk and Robert Slutzky) Design of a mental health centre for the Jewish Counselling and Service Agency, West Orange, New Jersey Improvement project for the Hoboken Center Waterfront Smith House, Darien, Connecticut (completed in 1967)
1966	Hoffmann House, East Hampton, New York (completed in 1967)
1967	Saltzman House, East Hampton, New York (completed in 1969) Westbeth artists' residence, Greenwich Village, New York (completed in 1970)
1968	Institute for health and physical education in State University College, Fredonia, New York (completed in 1972)
1969	Bronx Urban Development Plan, New York National Honor Awards Prize from the American Institute of Architects (AIA, and won again in 1971 and 1974)
1969	House at Old Westbury, New York (completed in 1971)
1969	Monroe Developmental Center, Rochester, New York (completed in 1974) Twin Parks Northeast Residences, Bronx, New York
1970	Bronx Developmental Center, Bronx, New York (completed in 1977) Prototype of buildings for offices and laboratories for the Olivetti Branch Offices, Irvine, Minneapolis, Boston, Brooklyn, Patterson Accommodation project for the Olivetti Training Center, Tarrytown, New York Project for the central headquarters of Olivetti Corporation, North America, Fairfax, Virginia
1971	Douglas House Harbor Springs, Michigan (completed in 1973) Maidman House, Sands Point, New York (completed in 1976)
1972	Shamberg House, Chappaqua, New York (completed in 1974)
1973	Project for residences at Paddington Station, New York Project for a modern art museum at Villa Strozzi, Florence Resident architect at the American Academy in Rome Exhibited at the 15th Triennale di Milano
1974	Project for residential block Yonkers, New York Project for student accommodation at Cornell University, Ithaca, New York
1975	Bishop's Chair at Yale University

	Project for a rehabilitation unit at Bronx Psychiatric Center, Bronx, New York

Project for a rehabilitation unit at Bronx Psychiatric Center, Bronx, New York
Design for the Theatrum, New Harmony, Indiana
Ceramic workshop for Sarah Campbell Blaffer, New Harmony, Indiana (completed in 1978)
The Atheneum, New Harmony, Indiana (completed in 1979)

1976   Participated in the Venice Biennial
Prototype project for a suburban house, Concord, Massachusetts
Alamo Plaza Project, Colorado Springs, Colorado
Preparation of the inauguration exhibition of Cooper-Hewitt Museum, New York

1977   Project for Manchester Civic Center, Manchester, New Hampshire
Preparation of the New York School exhibition at the Design State Museum, Albany, New York
Aye Simon reading room in the Salomon R. Guggenheim Museum, New York,
(completed in 1978)

1978   Hartford Seminary, Hartford, Connecticut (completed in 1981)
Primary school in Clift Creek, Columbus, Indiana (completed in 1982)
Furniture for Knoll International
Museum of decorative arts, Frankfurt on Main, Germany (completed in 1985)

1979   Giovannitti House, Pittsburgh, Pennsylvania (completed in 1983)
Project for headquarters for Irwin Union Bank and Trust Company, Columbus, Indiana

1980   Building project for Somerset flats, Beverly Hills, California
Project for tender for a residential complex on 67th street, New York
Objects for Alessi Design
High Museum of Art, Atlanta, Georgia (completed in 1983)

1981   Project for registered headquarters of Renault, Boulogne Billancourt, France

1982   Des Moines Art Center, Des Moines, Iowa (completed in 1982)

1983   Tender for the Opera Bastille, Paris
Tender for redevelopment of the Lingotto site, Turin
Central headquarters of Siemens, Munich, Germany (completed in 1988)
Furniture objects for Swid-Powell Designs (up to 1996)

1984   Pritzker Prize
Barnum Museum, Bridgeport, Connecticut
House at Westchester, New York (completed in 1986)
Ackerberg House, Malibu, California (extended in 1993-1995)
Bridgeport Center, Bridgeport, Connecticut (completed in 1989)
Grotta House, Harding Township, New Jersey
Offices and laboratories for Siemens, Munich, Germany (completed in 1990)

1985   Getty Center, Los Angeles, California (completed in 1997)

1986   Studio of Richard Meier & Partners, New York
Studio of Richard Meier & Partners, Los Angeles
Tender for the Supreme Court Headquarters, Jerusalem, Israel
Building for exhibitions and conferences in Ulm, Germany (completed in 1993)

1987   Project for the headquarters of the National Investment Bank, The Hague
Tender for the Santa Monica Beach Hotel, Santa Monica, California
Tender for the renovation of Madison Square Garden, New York
Museum of Contemporary Art, Barcelona
Weishaupt Forum, Schwendi, Germania (completed in 1992)
Central headquarters of the Royal Dutch paper mills, Hilversum, Holland

1988   Central headquarters of Canal +, Paris
Residential complex, Espace Pitôt, Montpellier
Plans for Antwerp harbour and administration centre, Antwerp
RIBA gold medal

1989   Project for the headquarters of the company CMB, Antwerp
        Project for office tower-block for Quandt, Frankfurt on Main
        Tender for the Bibliothèque de France, Paris
        Research centre for Daimler-Benz, Ulm, Germany (completed in 1993)
        Hypolux Bank, Luxembourg (completed in 1993)
        Town hall and national library, The Hague, Holland (completed in 1995)

1990   Camden Hospital, Singapore (completed in 1999)

1991   Rachofsky House, Dallas, Texas (completed in 1996)
        Swissair North America, Melville, New York (completed in 1994)

1993   Federal Court Islip, New York (completed in 2000)

1994   Radio and TV Museum, Beverly Hills, California (completed in 1996)
        Gagosian Art Gallery, Beverly Hills

1995   Neugebauer House, Naples, Florida (completed in 1998)
        Sandra Day O'Connor Federal Court, Phoenix, Arizona (completed in 2000)
        Ara Pacis Museum, Rome (completed in 2006)

1996   Dio Padre Misericordioso Church, Rome (completed in 2004)

1998   Large warehouse for Peek & Cloppenburg, Düsseldorf (completed in 2001)
        Richmers central headquarters, Hamburg (completed in 2001)
        Bridge project for Cittadella sul Panaro, Alessandria (completed in 2006)
        Canon central headquarters, Tokyo (completed in 2002)

1999   House at Malibu, California (completed in 2001)
        Tower blocks for flats in 173-176 Perry Street, New York (completed in 2002)

2001   Landscape improvement plan and project for show arena, Bethel, New York
        Frieder Burda Museum, Baden Baden, Germany (completed in 2004)
        Art history library at Yale University, New Haven, Connecticut (completed in 2005)

2002   Restaurant 66 Leonard Street, New York (completed in 2003)

2003   Residences in Jesolo (completed in 2007)

2007   Project for 3 tower blocks for residences, hotel and flats in Jesolo (work in progress)

Works

Marzia Marandola wrote the texts for the "Works"
and "Projects" sections

Smith House
Darien, Connecticut, Usa, 1965-1967

above
View from the east, from the coastal inlet

opposite page
Planimetry

Smith House is a promotional, programmed manifestation; its delicate geometries wrapped in nature carry the international success of Meier, the fantastic creator of houses. It is the type of building against which he repeatedly measured himself throughout the first decade of his career. Situated on a small hill along the jagged coastline of Connecticut nestled among rocks, sand and pine trees, Smith House seems to rest on the curves of the land. Its compact form empties out onto the cliff's facade as well as a corner overlooking a small beach in such a way as to project the interior out to its natural surroundings. Situated on the opposite side, the entrance is a green pathway that leads to the garage. Here, the path stops and leads to an access ramp that brings to the main floor. Meier's methodology took root in this project. His design projects are centred on architectural components – entrances, flow, functional layout, structure, enclosures – elements that mutate in space and form via creative fusion.

In Smith House, the floor plan is a strictly white prism comprising two rectangles, which are parallel to the topographic axes of the site. On the corners of the diagonal the windowless stair block – which joins the three interior levels – and the sinuous sculptural exterior ramp – which leads from front lawn to first floor – are detached. Arranged on three levels, the layout is characterised by a definite separation between common and private areas. In the former, the spectacular double height lounge features large windows that allow the light and colours of nature to penetrate. More intimate and cosy, the private area houses bedrooms and bathrooms. In these rooms, the wood walls give way to small yet refined quadrangular windows. This separation of living quarters into day zone and night zone is further emphasised by the positioning of the support structures. The open-plan area, projected onto the landscape, is sustained by four steel columns, positioned farther back with respect to the glazed outline, its clean surface broken by the trimmed parallelepiped of the brick fireplace. In the bedroom areas, the wood walls are positioned along the axis of the support structures. Though the residence is clearly marked by this split between day zone and night zone and the net difference between them in terms of materials and construction techniques, both areas brim with charm and elegance. The northwest entrance is enigmatic and introvert while the southeast portion is ornamental and spectacular.

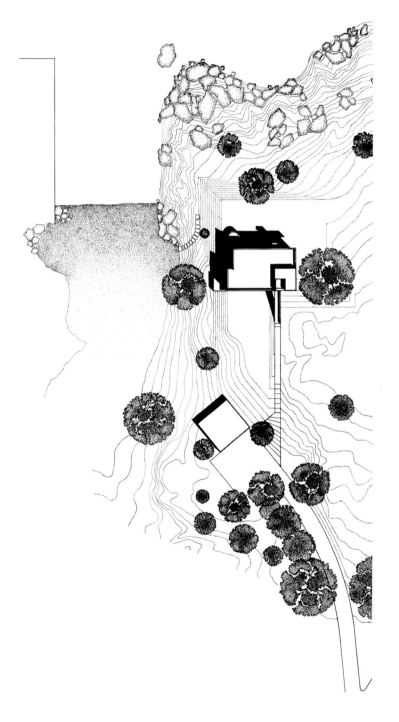

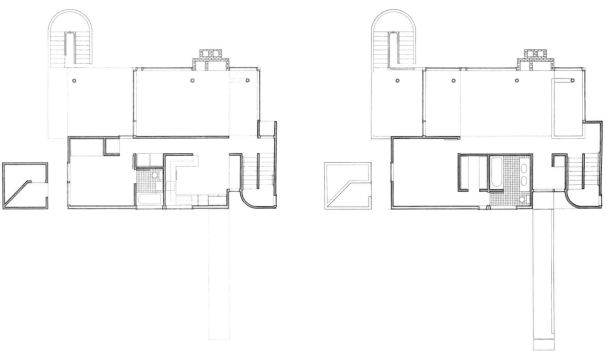

From the top, living room
on the first floor toward
the east and southwest

opposite page
above
Nocturnal view from
the south
below
Ground floor and first floor
layout

The Atheneum

New Harmony, Indiana, Usa, 1975-1979

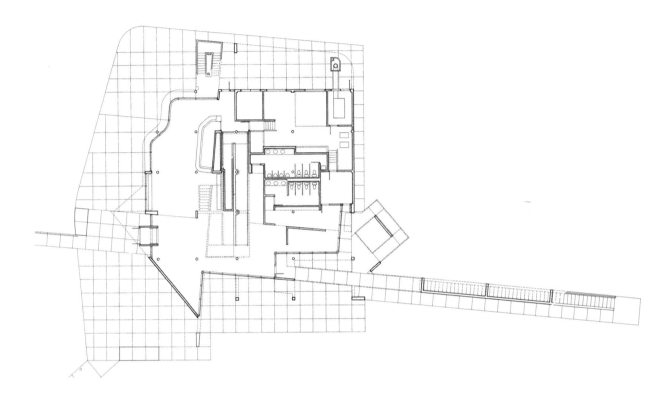

Ground floor layout

New Harmony is testimony to 18th-century social utopias. It was founded in 1814 as a self-sufficient, ideal community. Following various misfortunes, which included the leadership of Robert Owen, it fell to ruin and was abandoned until the 1960s, when it was completely renovated. Since then, it has been welcoming those who are seeking harmony with nature. The restructuring project included: the construction of a chapel (1959-1961), designed by Philip Johnson (1906-2005); a hotel as well as the rebuilding of the auditorium (late 1960s) after a design by Evans Woollen; a ceramic workshop (1975-1978) and the documentation centre and

Atheneum Welcome Centre, planned by Meier. Reachable by boat, it rises up like a temple on an artificial hill that provides an embankment against the periodic flooding of the Wabash. The building consists of two overlapping grids, one of which replicates the orthogonal network of the original 18th-century structure while the other alludes to the diagonality of the nearby urban suburbs. In the former, the transversal axis connects the building to the river docking area, from where visitors arrive to the village, landing at the opposite front. From there, a monumental ramp accesses the first floor. The Atheneum is characterised by Meier's extraordinary ability to

distinguish and emphasise spatial and hierarchical differences, altering interiors through a sophisticated and undogmatic use of continuous and curvilinear enclosures, structural lattices and pathways that communicate with the exterior. These elements serve to breathe life into otherwise inanimate spaces, also creating symbolic facets and an astonishing kaleidoscope, with colours determined by variations in lighting. From the ground floor, which houses the information booths and the exhibition rooms, a sculptured ramp winds up to the floor above, where the auditorium as well as additional halls are situated. The conference

room and the spectacular, panoramic roof terrace are located o the third floor.

The Atheneum building cannot be summed up as a simple piece of geometry. It derives from an intertwining of assembled buildings on a communal quadrangular plan, cast on a matrix of blended lines with continuous fractures and a hyperbolic sequence of spatial events. With its elusive, altering outline, the building is a blend of latticed planes that interplay with glossy surfaces of snow-white sheets of porcelain steel. The result is a fairy-tale image; a stranded boat or Atlantic liner, stranded on a hill and berthed among the trees.

View from the southeast wirth front entrance

page 40
From the top, internal main ramp and north-south section

page 41
View of the entrance ramp from the east

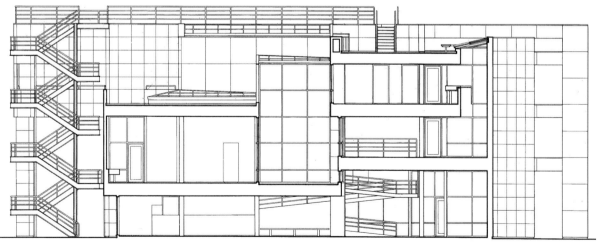

41

Museum of Applied Art
Frankfurt, Germany, 1979-1985

The Metzler Villa
and the new museum
seen from the river

Winning the contract to extend the Museum of Applied Art in Frankfurt, Germany, was key to Meier's career, as he was then required to construct for the first time in Europe, where until then he had only designed the Museum of Modern Art (1973) in the mews of Villa Strozzi in Florence. Moreover, in Frankfurt it was not an issue of simply creating a museum, a building type particularly congenial to the architect, as much as it was to converse with an urban scale museum system, which upgraded the banks of the Main from a residential to a public area. Meier had to organise the extension of Villa Metzler, an 18th-century pavilion, which had by then become insufficient for the collection. The plan distributed the new buildings in an assembly of spaces ordered

on two Cartesian grids, rotated a few
degrees with respect to a common vertex,
which coincides with Villa Metzer, and thus
became the focus of the project, determining
one of the orientation systems of the new
pavilions and the design module of the
additional structure. The other orientation
system was determined by the river which
guided the walkways and the open spaces.
The two superimposed grids discipline the
hierarchy of the walkways and control the
system of the extension which, around a
square garden, extends over three blocks in
an L shape, completing a quadrangular plot
perfectly, deduced by the multiples of the
almost cubic volume of Villa Metzer, the side
of which is around 18 metres, and becomes
the module which, on plan and erected,
regulates the new buildings.

The snow-white external walls, which have
alternating plaster and panels of strictly
white porcelain steel, are in a lattice design
with thick, glazed, modular grills, grafted
by cubes of concrete-framed glass blocks,
broken down by deep cuts, elements
which open up the architecture to the
natural landscape.

The museum is entered from the ground
floor via a hall, which introduces the
temporary exhibitions, the administrative
offices and the outdoor bar/restaurant in the
internal garden. The visitor's walkway
proceeds via a spectacular ramp which,
leaning against the glazed perimeter, leads
to the upper floors, building up to an
exceptional architectural experience; a walk
which reveals the building and allows the
discovery of the exhibited works at different
angles, until reaching the upper rooms
reserved for the permanent exhibitions.

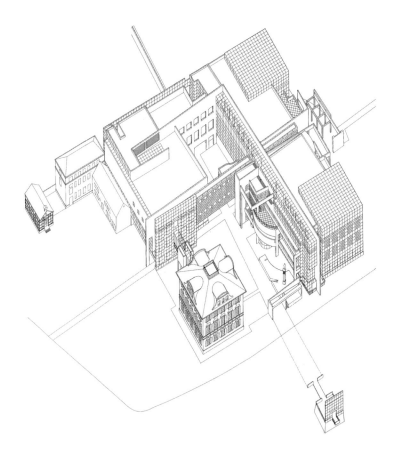

Axonometric plan
of the complex with
the Metzler Villa

page 44
From the top, southwest
view, section along the
courtyards toward the
Metzler Villa and façade
with ramps and windows
counterposed to the villa

page 45
Internal ramps

J. Paul Getty Center for the Fine Arts
Los Angeles, California, Usa, 1984-1997

Center for the History
of Art and the Humanities

The Getty Center, the wealthy foundation for the history of art, was founded by Paul Getty (1892-1976), the Minneapolis oil magnate and avid collector who started collecting in the 1930s and acquired and collected numerous works of art in Los Angeles. Getty commissioned a villa in the style of the architecture of Pompei (1970-1974) from the design studio of Bob Langdon and Ernie Wilson for his increasingly larger collection which quickly showed itself to be insufficient. Getty then left part of his estate for an arts centre which, subject to winning the tender, was commissioned to Richard Meier. This was not for a museum but for a citadel for the study and preservation of the works of art; an acropolis of culture which Meier modelled on

Villa Adriana and the gardens of Villa d'Este in Tivoli and Villa Lante in Bagnaia. Built over an area of 45 hectares in the area of Brentwood, the Getty Center dominates the Santa Monica Mountains and the urban network of Los Angeles. As usual it was the site which gave Meier the idea for the generating grids of the design, deduced from the pattern of the San Diego Freeway, which runs towards San Fernando Valley, curving by 22.5 degrees. The buildings which curl around the exhibition pavilions of the Getty Museum are divided around a courtyard governed by the motorway layout, parallel to the ridges of the hills, whereas on the crossover axis there is the auditorium with the information centre, the restaurant-café, and the circular body of the Center for the History of Art and the Humanities. This imposing architectural emergence contains the library with more than a million books, archives, studies, offices, and seminary rooms. Visitors reach the entrance via a silent, white tram, guided on a central axis. Leaving the auditorium, Art History Information Program and Conservation Institute to the left, and the restaurant-cafe to the right, the museum courtyard is reached, where a collection of European art, from the medieval period to the late 18th century, is distributed in pavilions. Photographs and manuscripts are kept on the lower floors, where there is less natural light, while the upper rooms, illuminated by box-shaped skylights, display the paintings. The axis of the museum courtyards extends into the landscape via a ramped belvedere leaning on a wing of rustic travertine, and concludes with a circular bulwark, also in rustic travertine, which surrounds the spectacular cactus garden suspended over the Los Angeles metropolis. All the buildings are dazzling white. Meier's typical wall covering of porcelain steel alternates with open-jointed sheets in slot-vented Italian travertine, which enhances the corrugated materialness of the Roman stone and historically attests to the public prestige of the architecture. The angled geometries of the walkways are softened by overflowing curvaceous structures, which take up position as an orographic, visual connection of the various building units. Designed by Robert Irwin, who slightly modified Meier's design, the gardens were laid and

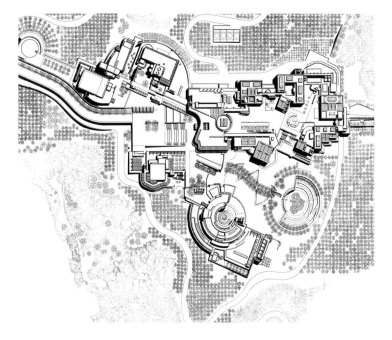

Overall layout

planted between 1992 and 1997, combining different species. The central garden, onto which the Center for the History of Art and the museum pavilions face, is concluded downhill with a layout which replicates the plans of the Center for The History of Art in the form of a circular theatre of vegetation descending down three levels towards the central expanse of water, where there are concentric circles of trees. In a decision that was as random as it was enigmatic, the Getty Trust commissioned the interiors to Thierry Despont, the trendy French-American decorator from New York, whose ideas, according to what Meier wrote in *Building the Getty* (1999), did not tie in with those of the designer.

47

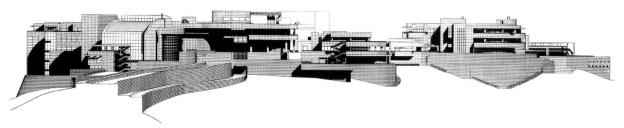

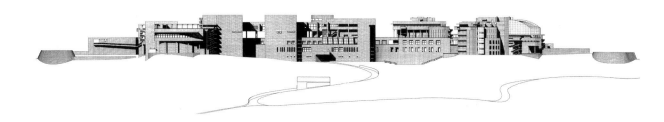

From the top, entrance
to the museums, internal
ramp system and Ancient
Art exhibition halls

opposite page
From the top, Center
for the History of Art
and the Humanities,
north view of the entrance
and east section seen
from the valley

Museum of Contemporary Art
Barcelona, Spain, 1987-1996

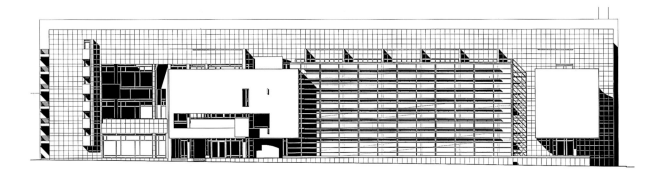

Main façade overlooking the square

The Museum of Contemporary Art in Barcelona was one of Meier's first projects dealing with a consolidated, dense urban context such as the historical centre of Barcelona, gravitating on the Casa de la Caritat. As is usual for Meier, it was the site that gave him the idea for the alignments of the new building which, narrow in the thick woven area of the Gothic quarter, is set on a rectangular base and is similar to that of the nearby Caritat cloister. The plan of the Museum seems to exalt the spatial assembly of the monastery, so much so that the church facility, with a hall featuring a semi-circular apse, is traceable in the extended facility of the museum, which is concluded with a circular structure. The building unit looks compact and unitary, but actually constitutes the juxtaposition of three structures: an extended parallelepiped with large exhibition rooms and offices, restoration workshops and bar at the back, a cylindrical structure housing the entrance and vertical connections, and finally an end structure,

hollowed out as if holding the impression of the adjacent cylinder of the hall for exhibiting small objects. The three structures are joined by a thick façade which looks onto the square. On the exterior fronts, level shifts, growths of cylindrical structures and various curves put architecture into action, emphasising the entrances and the perspective pivots of the roads that lead to the museum. The basic characteristics of Meier's repertoire can also be found in this work: high vestibules, scenographic, rope ramps, crossed views, almost totally windowless exterior fronts, which converse with completely glazed walls, and an imperative use of the colour white. From the opposite square, la Plaça des Angels, the Museum can be entered via a double ramp, almost concealed by the base block, which, leaning on the main front in parallel, anticipates the spectacular internal ramp illuminated by roof skylights and, visible via the glazed wall, unfurls aerially between the three levels of exhibition rooms.

Façade and entrance seen from the east

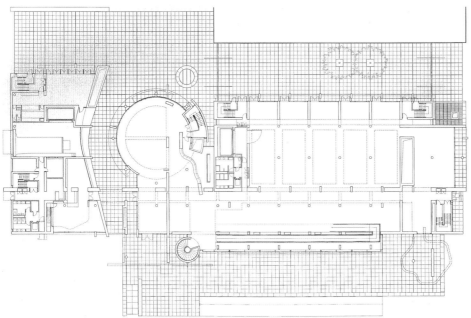

Ramp seen from the entrance

side
Ground floor layout

side
Ramp seen from
the last floor

below
Layout of the first floor

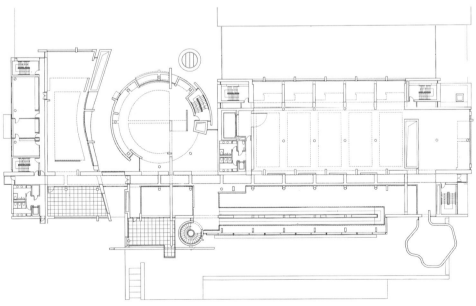

Neugebauer House
Naples, Florida, Usa, 1995-1998

Planivolumetry

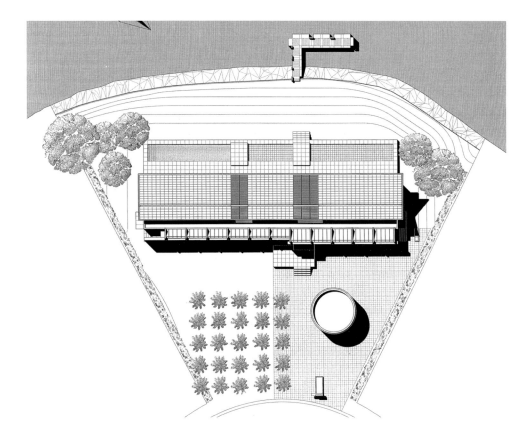

Neugebauer House deviates from Meier's usual production, whereby the house has the demonstrative theme of his *ars aedificatoria*. Striking landscape surrounds the 6000 sq.m plot at Doubloon Bay. The entrance is emphasised by a palm grove, with an orthogonal pattern that contrasts with the cylindrical geometry of the garage. On a rectangular podium space, as with all Meier's houses, space is characterised by communal areas, unfolding onto the marine panorama, and the private areas that curl behind the front

of the entrance. The sequence of the rooms, aligned on a directrix of 85 metres, parallel to the shore, allows all the rooms to open onto the sea. The house is actually a giant asymmetrical, inverted, double pitch roof, supported by a steel frame, which, a unique case in Meier's houses, secures its image and declares the mutual relationship between space and structure. Distributed on one level, the rectangular plan and the distinct longitudinal fronts are all anomalous: the front toward the sea is transparent and set by the structure; the

entrance front, closed and compact, is covered with light stone sheets, notched with vertical slits and crowned by a continuous slot which intercepts the roof skylight. Access, in addition to being possible from the long fronts, is also possible at the ends, in correspondence with a perimeter service corridor. The main entrance axis intersects longitudinal space fascias: first of all the service corridor, housing the rooms and the wardrobes, then a communal lobby that leads to the living room/dining room. Finally there is the long passage which,

screened by *brise-soleil,* reconnects all the rooms on the seafront. From this side the base plate extends out like a *parvis*, and is trimmed by a layer of rectangular water, which can be crossed via two stone slabs. The house is imbued with allusions to the history of architecture: from the verbal parsimony of Mies van der Rohe to the light chamber of the Baroque builders, whereas the rectangle that commands the lengthwise distribution of the rooms states explicit homage to the houses of the master Marcel Breuer.

Façade toward
Doubloon Bay

page 57
Lateral façade
and transversal section

pagina 58
Living room and
longitudinal section

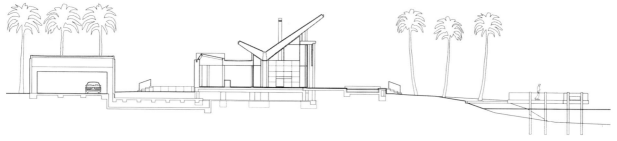

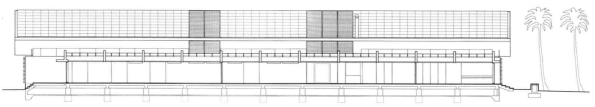

Sandra Day Federal Courthouse

Phoenix, Arizona, Usa, 1995-2000

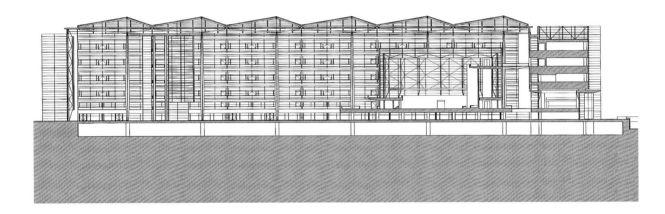

Longitudinal section

Bordered to the North by Washington Street, Jefferson Street to the South, Fourth Avenue to the East and Seventh Avenue to the West, the Federal Court, with the square and garden (not yet completed) occupies a good three blocks of the orthogonal network of Phoenix. Neighbouring Dodge Theatre, it is situated between the political and business areas, in the heart of downtown.
Designed at the same time as the Ara Pacis Museum, the Jubilee Church, and Neugebauer House, it shares the same innovation. First of all, the simple geometry,

which guides the rectangular plan measuring 105 by 45 metres, with a height of 6 floors, is literally determined by the pattern of the block and its exposure to the sun, decisive in the torrid climate of Arizona. These constraints also determined the difference and hierarchy of the facades, unusual until then for Meier.
As is usual in Meier's work, the architecture arises from the dialectic harmony of two contrasting bodies: an aerial, transparent parallelepiped, the walls of which spread to the North and East, protected by the fierce

southern and western sun by an L-shaped body, screened by a continuous, internal wall. Transparent and opaque, collective and individual, fluent and divided, are the opposing pairs which govern the project. In the L-shaped opaque block there are the judges' offices, the press room, 19 judicial rooms, the library, and the cafeteria; rooms which are accessed by galleries facing onto the glazed rectangular square, where the spatial sound is reminiscent of both the Gothic cathedral and Palm House. This covered square, which is bright and air-conditioned, partially due to low cost passive technology similar to that of the Ara Pacis Museum, is focused on a monumental glazed cylinder which, being the heart of the building, contains the special judicial rooms. The entrance is characterised on the eastern front by a canopy supported on four steel pillars, which summarises the figurativeness of the building, skilfully as much as it is exclusively deviated by the steel structure of the elegant branched pillars, the grills of the wall covering panels and the saw tooth glass which designs the brash, cuspate profile of the roof.

Nocturnal view from Washington Street

page 60
From the top, layout of the ground floor and interior of a special courtroom within the cylindrical body

page 61
Interior toward the entrance hall

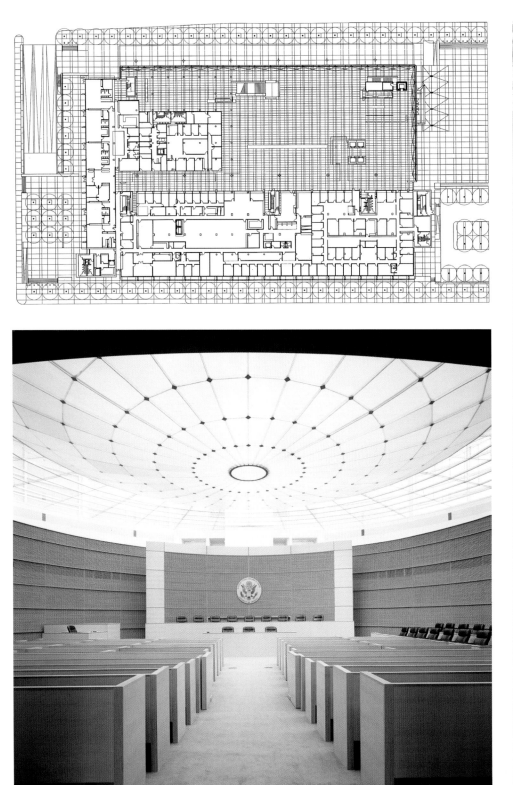

Dio Padre Misericordioso Church and Parish Centre

Tor Tre Teste, Rome, Italy, 1996-2003

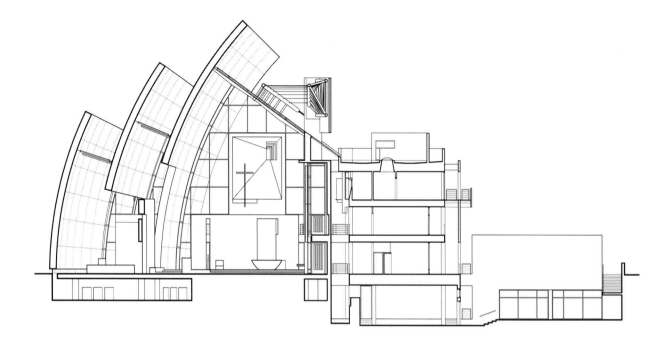

Section toward the main altar

The Vicariate of Rome issued an international invitation to tender (1995) for the design of a parish centre in the area of Tor Tre Teste. Though he had never designed churches, Meier won the tender. A main requisite of the project was that it had to celebrate, with visual immediacy and spatial significance, the 2000 Jubilee as well as Catholicism and Rome as "a place of welcome." Meier responded with an explosive design in which he skilfully employed light – a fundamental component of Christian symbology – combined with highly expressive and bold technological solutions. As usual, he masterminded his plan by using

the site as inspiration. He contemplated the irregular plot, delimited by a large park and trimmed by the branching off of the road, which animates the area and extends to the building, marking spatial continuity between the built-up area, the park, and the church. The latter assumes an urban, symbolic pre-eminence, analogous to the historical churches in the centre. Ultimately, the project was sectioned in two: the area of worship and a parish centre. A gentle rotation of the worship block topographically underlines the distinction between the two components, emphasised by dramatic choices.

Meier here adopted a design strategy that had already been tested in projects for houses and museums. Essentially, his usual elements – entrances, walkways, deliberate solutions of purpose, structure and enclosures – find powerful expression in this project, attaining a spectacular harmony between the perforated, geometrical curves and the area of worship, delimited by three amazing "shells," and the orthogonal, opaque area that governs the parish centre, drastically restructured compared to the original. Sliced into spheres of equal radius, the three shells enveloping the area of worship discretely allude to the mystery of the Holy Trinity and the Christian symbol of water, while directing the gaze of the congregation toward the sky, beyond the glazed slope of the hall. The overall white, visionary spatiality required formidable technical mastery in terms of processes required for bleaching the anti-pollution concrete as well as assembling the gigantic, reinforced concrete structures. In fact, the latter dominate and control the three oversize sails, which immediately captured the imagination and fancy of the Romans, making Meier's church a true icon of the new neighbourhood.

Nocturnal view
of the front apse

63

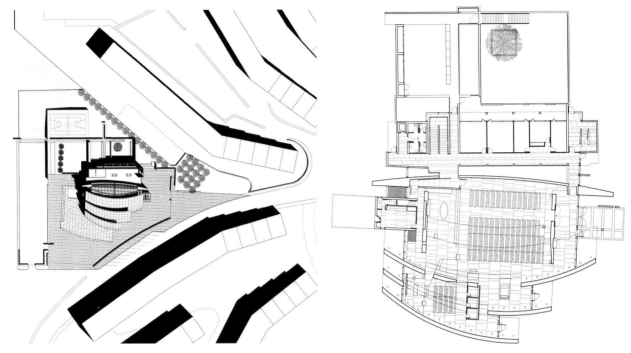

From the top, overall
planimetry of the Tor Tre
Teste neighbourhood
with church, plan of the
church and parish centre
and view of the nave
toward the entrance wall

opposite page
Nave looking toward
the main altar

Ara Pacis Museum
Rome, Italy, 1995-2006

Main entrance

Commissioned by the Mayor of Rome, Francesco Rutelli, in 1995, the museum was ideated for the purpose of exhibiting a unique work of architectural proportions: the Ara Pacis. A magnificent decorated altar, Ara Pacis was erected by the Roman Senate around 9 B.C. to celebrate Emperor Augustus, peacemaker of the Empire. In addition to the exhibition space reserved for this piece of art, the new building hosts a small auditorium, a restaurant-café with a panoramic terrace, a bookshop and, on the ground floor, offices and rooms for educational exhibitions. The museum, which replaces a pavilion originally built in the 1930s and conveniently demolished, was raised on a narrow plot of land (120 metres in length) in the heart of Rome, between the Lungotevere and Piazza

Augusto Imperatore, where there are the remains of the mausoleum of Augustus. Inaugurated on the anniversary of the birth of Augustus, 23rd September 2005, and opened to the public on the Birth of Rome commemoration, 21st April 2006, the museum sparked controversy due to its supposed extraneousness to the context of the town. Causing a scandal are the immaculate white of its panelled walls in recycled white glass, which seems to be a provocation to the plaster and brick in the city, and the stereometric purism of the three blocks, two opaque head blocks and a transparent block at the centre which, joined to the hovering roof level, articulate the building.

Entry is from a raised square which invites the visitor to contemplate the architecture, the water from the fountain, and the facades of two Renaissance churches facing the museum. Roman construction tradition is evoked by a wall that, in open-jointed slabs of slot-vented travertine, penetrates the entrance and introduces the contemplation of the Ara, shutting out the daily noise and frenzy of the Lungotevere. Inside, the light which is skilfully regulated by the architecture, bathes the white walls, shines on the smoothed travertine surfaces and its soft marble reliefs of the Ara. It creates a suspended, metaphysical atmosphere, where

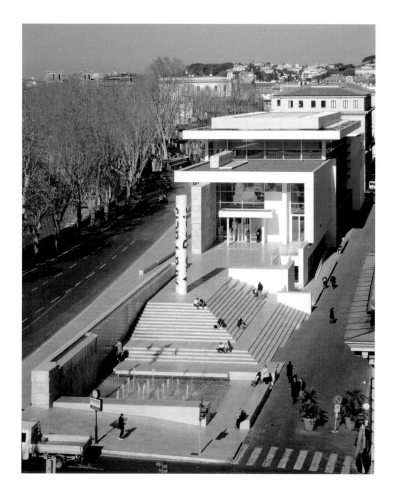

the changing of natural light scans the passage of time, and the city, beyond the glass of the *brise-soleil*, dialogues via the art with its ancient history, symbolised by the altar of Augustus, exposed like a gem in a crystal case.

Aerial view of the entrance with staircase and fountain

67

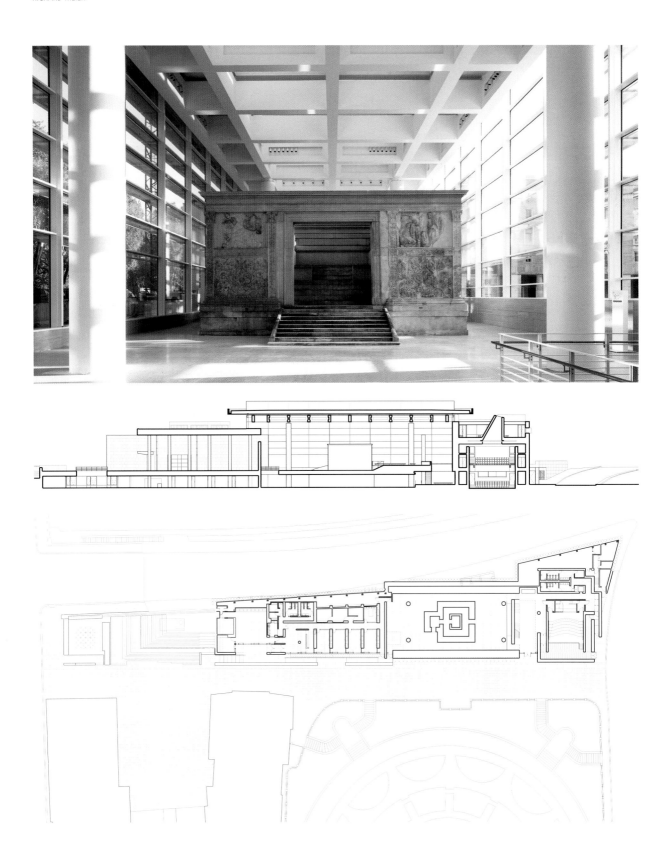

Hall of mosaics seen
from the upper level

opposite page
Interior with Ara Pacis
by Augustus, longitudinal
section seen from the
Mausoleum of Augustus
and overall planimetry
of the project whit axes

West Village Towers
New York, Usa, 1999-2006

Planimetry of the three towers with prospects over West Street

This luxurious residential complex in Greenwich Village is the first project Meier ever carried out in Manhattan. Arranged on sixteen floors, it comprises three tower blocks. The first two are situated on the North and South corners of Perry Street and West Street while the third faces Charles Street. It is part of the City's improvement plan for the river front overlooking New Jersey and includes the new Hudson River Park, a network of gardens that comprises sports and recreation centres and extends from Battery Park City to 59th Street.

The tower blocks, designed to favour and take advantage of the spectacular views of the river and Manhattan, have, as is always the case in Meier's architectures, a double structure. Continuous and box-like in the concrete lift block, which protrudes onto the Eastern side, this is the least panoramic edifice. It comprises circular pillars in the wells, which allowed utmost freedom in terms of layout and made it possible to maximise window space.
Protected by thermal glass panels, the windows feature frames characterised by a

The three towers seen from the Hudson

geometric form that commands the minimalist layout of the facades.

The tower blocks on Perry Street each house apartments at every level. Anchored to a trapezoidal base, the northern block is the slimmest and measures 170 sq.m. These apartments have one or two bedrooms while the southern block apartments are larger, with two or three bedrooms. In both blocks the bedrooms are located on the eastern side, away from the river and have a less interesting view.

More panoramic, the facades facing west are marked by an oblique layout. Meier has here masterfully capitalised on the on the alignment with West Street, favouring both function and aesthetics. Each apartment has two corner terraces overlooking West Street. Ideated to serve as outdoor extensions of the living room, they boast a view to both the south and the west of the city and, hence, over Manhattan as well as the Hudson River. The third tower block, with has two identical apartments on each floor, is also characterised by its continuous glass exterior.

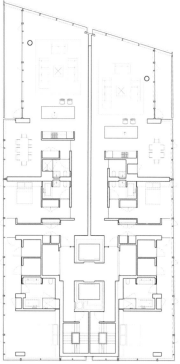

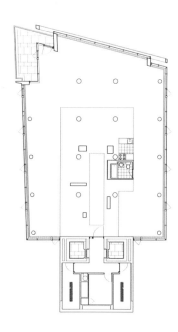

From the top, views from
corner living rooms of the
tower overlooking Charles
Street and of the one over
Perry Street

opposite page
From the top, three towers
seen from the river in the
background of the Village
and typical floor plans
of the three buildings

Richard Meier Model Museum
New York, Usa, 2007

above and opposite page
General views
of the interior

Located in Queens, NY, nestled between now unused industrial buildings and plants, the Richard Meier Model Museum Meier is an exceptional venue created by Meier to preserve and host his sculptures of studios. Archives of his drawings and documents are located along with his sculptures in a building with a strong industrial favour on the outside, its windows boasting an extraordinary view of Manhattan. L-shaped, the museum is dotted by rustic cement pillars. The external wall, with its oversize windows, is characterised by exposed tubing and, as is typical of the master's architectures, everything is in white intonaco or paint. Meier has not greatly altered the original structure, limiting his project to the addition of

an accurate and intentional use of natural and artificial lighting paired with sophisticated igrometric system, which guarantee the materials' perfect preservation. Covering 340 sq.m, the exhibition area contains approximately 300 models, of varying sizes but mostly in wood, of the Getty Center. This was the project that undeniably required the vastest range and greatest amount of models. They include specimens that display extensive sections of the Los Angeles area as well as a large scale model of one of the museum's halls. Small, plastic sculptures of his first villas of the 1960s, such as Smith House as well as his incomplete project for the World Trade Center in Manhattan, are but a handful of the many

models exhibited in a simple and didactic space, which was nonetheless specially ideated at creating a subtle but memorable impression. The masterful grouping and seemingly casual arrangement of the three-dimensional objects is reminiscent of style that so characterised London architect John Soane (1753-1837). Here, however, the fragments of Greek and Roman antiquity typical of Soane, have been replaced by the sharp steel sculptures and the wood, plastic and plaster sculptures moulded by their maker. As was habit in Soane's studio, the Meier Museum is open to students and aficionados of architecture interested in furthering their knowledge of the master's oeuvres. Meier confesses that the purpose of this collection is closely bound to its use outside the realm of his studio. The models are arranged on metal shelves, in an intriguing manner centred on a unique manipulation of shapes and lights, or on pedestals within display cases or even secured to the walls with visible rods – as is the case with the many sculptures, smelted by Meier himself. He in fact practiced sculpture in his youth. Spartan chairs, also designed by the architect, are available to visitors of the museum, allowing them to slowly enjoy and meditate upon the works on display, perhaps leafing through the books that depict the actual architectures and serve as perfect guides to an archaeological, historic and artistic visit of Meier's work.

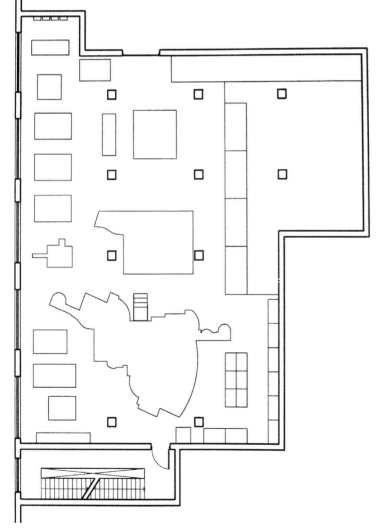

From the top, the exterior
of the industrial building
that houses the museum
and the layout of the first
floor with the arrangement
of the models

above
Interior with model
of J. Paul Getty Center
in the foreground

opposite page
Small scale models

Projects

Performing Arts Center

Bethel, New York, Usa, 2001

Located in Bethel, the Performing Arts Center is, in short, a landscape plan aimed at an artistic use of the site where the legendary Woodstock Festival took place in 1969. The project centred on creating walkways and communal areas equipped for artistic events and shows, in such a way as to capitalise on the natural beauty of the location.

A seductive element, the landscaped walkways converge in the Performing Arts Pavilion, a covered arena capable of hosting up to 14,000 spectators. Seats are arranged along the curves at each level creating an ancient semi-circular cavea, with the *scaenae frons* formed by the dressing rooms.

The geometric rigidity of the semi-circular terracing is counter-balanced by the corrugated lightness of the roof: a tubular, trellis structure upon which a corrugated laminboard, characterised by a flexible, ribbed outline.

Suspended on thin forks, the steel curtain technology protects the cavea and optimises the acoustics of the open space.

View of the theatre stalls toward the stage

opposite page
The large reticular roof amid the landscape

Jesolo Lido Project
Jesolo, Italy, 2003

Planimetry of the project
in the urban context

opposite page
From the top, transversal
section of the residences
and the various layouts

In 2003 the South Tyrolean company, Hobarg of Jesolo Lido, commissioned Meier a typically residential estate, to be constructed in phases in the seaside resort near to Venice. Between 2003 and 2007 the first residences, with 81 apartments and 3 shops, were completed behind the beach. Elegant and refined, the project was even awarded the prestigious Architettura Dedalo Minosse in 2008. Situated on opposite sides, the buildings overlook the council swimming pool and extend toward the road. A third building is scheduled for

completion in 2011 and will be raised in the area beyond the pine trees, on the beach. The edifice will be compact and its style will be in keeping with the white metallic partitions of the sunscreens, the marine fashion of the balconies and the enamelled steel stairways that characterise the already existent terraced houses. Meier's estate is part of an improvement project for the sea resort headed by the Kenzo Tange studio. Participating architects include Goncalo Byrne and Zaha Hadid and the landscape designer João Nunes.

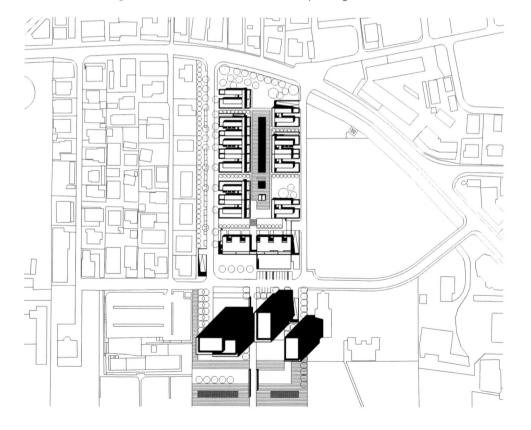

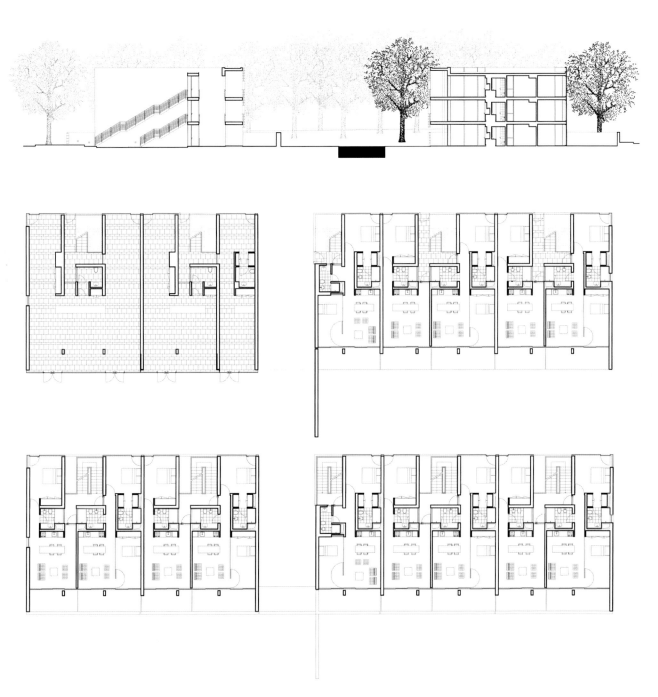

Italcementi's ITC Lab
Bergamo, Italy, 2005

Layout of the ground floor

The Italcementi laboratory is one of the buildings included in Jean Nouvel's master plan (2003) for Kilometro Rosso, the Science and Technology Park on the Milan-Venice motorway. After the successful collaboration for the Jubilee Church, Italcementi commissioned Meier for the construction of the building for laboratories, which includes offices, library, and social areas. Covering 11,000 sq.m, the V-shaped edifice descends two levels into the ground and rises two floors above ground. Each of its lateral facades are ordained, respectively, by the paths formed by the motorway ad the internal road system. The laboratories, which occupy 7500 sq.m, open onto the courtyard and are screened from the motorway by grills.

The front overlooking the road has a blind wall and a glazed wall delimiting the offices and the largest Italian library on cement. The vertex of the triangle is empty and comprises glazed full-height panels and cylindrical pillars, and the 20-metre overhang of the entrance canopy. The area flows to the inside, intersecting ramps and walkways, typical of Meier's style.

Novel addition to his architectural expression are the double front and the aerodynamic canopy of the roof. Constructed of anti-pollution cement, the building is energy efficient.

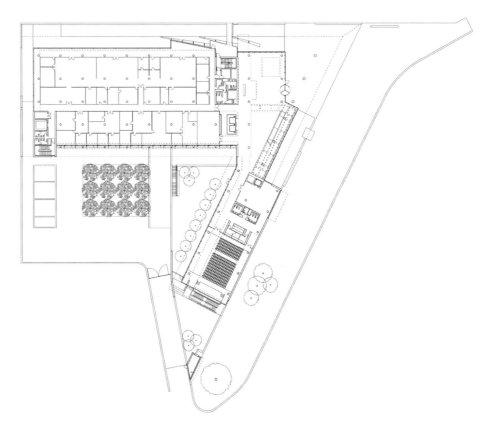

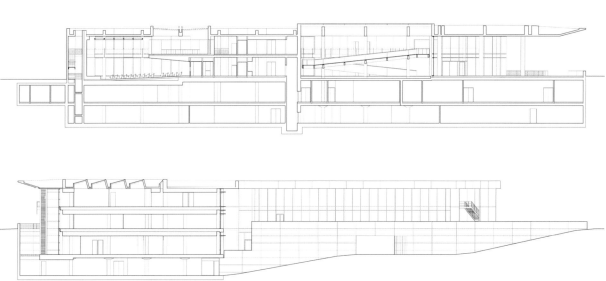

From the top, façade
overlooking internal road
and longitudinal sections

Thought

Niveo de Marmore

Preface

An ongoing conversation I have had with my children, Joseph and Ana, over the past year revolves around the question, "What is your favorite color?" Joseph, almost five years old, immediately responds, "Green," and when asked why, says, "Green is the color of grass, trees are green, green is all around us, it's the color of spring." Ana, who is three and doesn't like to be outdone by her brother, replies that her favorite color is blue, because "the sky is blue, the ocean is blue." Then both of them turn to me and say, "Daddy, what is your favorite color?" Every time we play this game, my response is the same: "White." "But Daddy," Joseph says, "you can't choose white. White is not a color; white is not in the rainbow; you have to choose a color that *is,* like red or green or blue or yellow." And I explain each time that I think white is the most wonderful color of all, because within it one can find every color of the rainbow.

White is in fact the color which intensifies the perception of all of the other hues that exist in natural light and in nature. It is against a white surface that one best appreciates the play of light and shadow, solids and voids. For this reason white has traditionally been taken as a symbol of purity and clarity, of perfection. Where other colors have relative values dependent upon their context, white retains its absoluteness. Yet when white is alone, it is never just white, but almost always some color that is itself being transformed by light and by everything changing in the sky, the clouds, the sun, the moon. Goethe said, "Color is the pain of light." Whiteness, perhaps, is the memory and the anticipation of color.

R. Meier, "Preface", in *Richard Meier: Architectures: 1964-1984,* New York: Rizzoli, 1984, pp. 8-9.

Royal Gold Medal Address

Basically that is what Post-Modernism was, a moving backwards. It was a process that took from original copies, copies of copies, imitations of interpretations, all timidly following the past. This not only ransacked our past, but more importantly robbed us of our present, obliterating our future. This overweening bid to be liked was in conflict with the true creative process. The crucial relationship between the creative mind and its time, the delicate balance between being of the culture and outside it cannot be subjected to narcissistic demands of consumerism.

I believe that the attempt by Post-Modernism to discredit rational thought, to attack reason and systematic analysis in order to argue for the comfort of quotation in which everything is arbitrary and accidental is over. Post-Modernism is an attitude of the past. Its folly is being replaced today by ordered logic, lucid clarity and an architecture which strives for the unique radiance of modernity.

The Modern Movement questioned this attitude of slavish re-creating of the past. It yanked architecture out of the padded yoke of popular opinion, out of the comfortable despair of the banal. It changed the way we look and think about architecture so that ideas about place, use, materials and technology are related to ideas about form, proportion, light and scale. In striving to broaden the morphogenetic field, technology became paramount. But it is as if in their love affair with the machine, with the cool light of the purely rational, they lost touch with the sensual, the ground of our aesthetic being. The heroic mind overwhelmed its own spiritual vision, for when the idea of the machine replaces the idea of the mind's eye and the architect's hand, there comes that deep alienation of man from his environment. Whereas the Modern masters seemed to our eyes to be too rigidly identified with the idea and potential of mass production, of industrial man, this is now a fact of life, simply one of a number of resources at the architect's disposal. We now assume the tectonic and spatial authority of the Modern Movement, each new miracle of building holds only limited fascination. For me, technology is no longer the subject of architecture, but simply the means. Architecture is the subject of my architecture.

Abstraction in architecture continues to be one of the most powerful legacies of the Heroic Period. It continues to provoke us to invent and to elaborate on ways to geometrically organise and interpret human activities. Distinct and completely evolved plastic systems such as De Stijl, Purism and Constructivism each embodied the thought that architecture was important and dealt with aspects of the machine and the poetry of space. Today, the most compelling extension of that impulse towards abstraction is Deconstructivism. I feel akin to the embrace of the purely sculptural. I applaud the evocative focus on intellectual commitment. However, the nature of their enquiry and the quality of their objects inevitably collide with my concerns for the particularities of scale and place. There is no place for the physical in the Decons' intriguing network of forces. The web of their universe exists in a mind clearly alienated from the hierarchy and order essential to habitation.

Nonetheless I defend the validity and vitality of their speculation on the unreal.

What I seek to do is to pursue the plastic limits of Modern Architecture to include a notion of beauty molded by light. My wish is to create a kind of spatial lyricism within the canon of pure form. Not too long ago someone asked me if I could choose the one building type that I preferred to do the rest of my life – what would it be? My answer was Museums.

Someone up there was listening, for I got my wish. My involvement with art and with museums has been lifelong. The whole issue of the relationship between art and the art of architecture is one that is of the deepest interest to me. The cross-references between art and architecture, which have always been important, are a very crucial part of my work.

Throughout history, artists have been thought of as shamans to the culture as a whole. In this priestly guise they were, and are, the messengers, the bringers of meaning, from the spiritual and the unconscious world. If one accepts this model of art as the delineation of the higher plane of being, then the museum, the container of the art, becomes the modern cathedral or sacred space. It

is the end of the pilgrimage whose root is the collective contemplation of the self, both cultural and spiritual. We are defended from our own unconscious, as the Deconstructivists point out the eruption of the irrational into life is alien or threatening. Religion as institution has clearly failed us. The elevation of art to the container and mediator to our higher selves is deeply significant. Besides the display of the actual art objects in the design of museums, the architecture has to deal with a set of fascinating relationships: the civic grandeur; the public experience; the relationship of the individual viewer to the individual object; the relationship of light to the object and to the viewer, as well as the relationship of the art and the space to the general surroundings. A museum in the twentieth century also has to deal with the new phenomenon of art as a consumer object and the concomitant vast numbers of consumers. Thus, the museum can be the quintessential expression of an architecture which is born out of the culture and yet is profoundly related to personal experience.

[…]

In the design of the museum, I am expanding and elaborating on what I consider to be the formal basis of the Modern Movement. What the twentieth century did was create the ability to crack open an otherwise Classically balanced plan. The spirit is allowed to go in and out through that crack, so that the experience of being in the museum is not static, but everchanging. Architecture is an art of substance, of materialised ideas about space. Between the demands of programme, site, locale, and building technology the architect has to find a means of making buildings communicate in the language of materials and textures. Buildings are for the contemplation of the eyes and mind, but also, no less importantly, to be experienced and savoured by all human senses.

You cannot have form in architecture which is unrelated to human experience; and you cannot approach an understanding of experience, in terms of architecture, without a strongly sensuous and tactile attitude toward form and space. The site invites the architect to search out a precise

and exquisitely reciprocal relationship between built architecture and natural topography.
This implies a harmony of parts, a rational procedure, a concern for qualities of proportion, a precision of detail, constructional integrity, programmatic appropriateness, and, not least, a respect for human scale. Besides an American attitude of openness, warmth, flexibility, and invention, my vision of the building also has to do with a more European-delivered, ideal of permanence, specificity and history. Architecture at its best is an integration of human scale, with civic grandeur, decorative simplicity with material richness, an interest in technical innovation with a respect for historical precedent. The essential urban dialogue takes place between type and incident, between public and private, between fabric and discontinuity, between history and the present moment. It is a dialogue that exists at every scale.
I believe it is possible to see my work as a sequence of investigations into the spatial interchange between public and private realms. This interchange expresses itself in varying conceptions but is always related in some way to a notion of architectural promenade, to an idea of passage.
My work is an attempt to find and re-define a sense of order; to understand, then, a relationship between what has been and what can be; to extract from our culture both the timeless and the topical. This, to me, ii the basis of style, the decision to include or exclude, choice, the final exercise of the individual will and intellect. Fundamentally, my meditations are on space, form, light and how to make them. The goal is presence, not illusion.
I pursue it with unrelenting vigour and believe that it is the heart and soul of architecture.

R. Meier, *RIBA Royal Gold Medal Address 1988*, 25 October 1988, in *Richard Meier Buildings and Projects 1979-1989*, London: Academy Editions,1990, pp. 211-214.

Preface

The relationship between art and the art of architecture is one that has always been of interest to me, and the intersections between them have been an intriguing route of investigation that I have visited and revisited throughout my career. Architecture is an art of substance. It is the materialization of ideas about space. Given the demands of program, site, locale, and building technology, the architect endeavors to make buildings communicate in the language of materials and textures. Architecture is for the contemplation of the eyes and the mind, but, no less important, it is to be experienced and savored by all human senses and synthesized by the mind. Designing a museum is one of the most liberating experiences available to an architect, one that expresses unique concerns for space, light, structure, and their interrelationship.
Though there are numerous requirements in the program of the museum, in my experience there are no norms or rules. If there are principles, they are principles that guide the relationship between the building and the works of art displayed within, the quality of the experience in relation to the works of art and the building context. If there are forces competing for attention in the design of museums, they involve the disparities between large-scale and smaller-scale objects.
In contemporary art, in particular, the size of canvas and sculpture has increased tremendously for certain artists.
The goal is to understand and communicate the scale relationship. I believe that different objects should be perceived in different ways. Yet, as an architect, one cannot assume in designing a space that a particular object will always be there. Most collections are periodically displaced, and the objects inhabiting the space change. Also important is the experience of being within the building. Visiting a museum is not an experience dedicated solely to the viewing of art.
In a museum, one sees people, and one sees to the outside.
And the museum is sited in a particular urban or natural environment, which is equally critical to the visitor's experience.
In creating various museum projects over the years, I have worked with the European and American tradition of spatial expression and of

J. Paul Getty Center for the Fine Arts, Los Angeles; nocturnal view of the entrance to the Center for the History of Art and the Humanities

curatorial philosophy, and what interests me is a synthesis of the two.

The Museum for the Decorative Arts in Frankfurt, in which light is a constant preoccupation, exemplifies the European notion of a museum, with windows and a building within a garden. At the Barcelona Museum of Contemporary Art, we were faced with a museum that did not have a permanent collection but would instead show traveling exhibitions as well as a collection that would begin to develop over time. For that we provided very flexible large galleries that could easily be adapted to accommodate all types and sizes of artwork. In America, the design of a museum is often analogous to a city in terms of its circulation. The museum is an urban experience made comprehensible by its organization, where the movement system is a viewing system.

As with any project, the site of the museum invites the architect to search out a precise and exquisitely reciprocal relationship between built form and natural topography. This implies a harmony of parts, a rational procedure, a concern for qualities of proportion, a precision of detail, constructional integrity, programmatic appropriateness, and, not least, a respect for human scale. At The Getty Center in Los Angeles, we designed galleries for a very specific collection, and spaces were specially created for the placement of unique and individual works of art, whether paintings, sculptures, or decorative-arts pieces.

The galleries therefore were quite fixed. From the start, it seemed that the only way to sensibly and responsibly design The Getty Center was to consider what was there, both the human-built city below and the natural land-forms surrounding the museum. As a function or both the rectilinear urban grid and the curvilinear forms of the site's contours, The Getty Center clearly stakes its place in the city of Los Angeles and in the Santa Monica Mountains.

The museum as a public destination must respond to this type of opportunity. It must be a place that is both introverted, insofar as its spaces are conducive to the contemplation of works of art, and that is also extroverted, insofar as its organization allows the visitor to experience its unique sense of place. Though Los Angeles has

Contemporary Art Museum, MACBA, Barcelona; interior walkways

of the circulation system through and around the buildings-all of that has to encourage a relaxed, open-ended sense of interaction.

In addition to what one might identify as the American attitude of openness, warmth, flexibility, and invention demonstrated in The Getty Center, my vision of museum architecture also addresses a more European ideal of permanence, specificity, and history.

Architecture at its best is an integration of human scale with civic grandeur, it is a combination of decorative simplicity with material richness, it is an expressed interest in technical innovation with a respect for historical precedent. The essential urban dialogue takes place between type and incident, between public and private, between the city's regular tissue and discontinuity, between history and the present moment. It is a dialogue that exists at every scale. I believe that the form of the city of the future is derived from the form of the city today.

As an architect who has struggled with the dense and often contradictory heritage of the European city, I have come to realize that there is no one answer or one idea that is the appropriate response to the question posed by an urban context. I would like to think that each individual situation can offer its own strategic lesson in urban contextuality.

Most of my European work has been conceived for highly problematic sites-at the heart of The Hague, in the shadow of the the Ulm Cathedral, in the Gothic Quarter of Barcelona. In each of these cases, the challenge was not simply to raise a building that could serve the prescribed cultural or corporate functions, but to integrate the new with the old in ways that would redefine an entire locale.

The issues presented by any historical context were magnified in the project for the new museum for the Ara Pacis, an altar dating to 9 B.C., in much the same way that issue of scale took on a unique dimension in he Getty Center. From the start, the city of Rome expressed a desire a protect and enhance Rome's cultural and monumental legacy and to promote town planning in the historical center of Rome, which

developed a reputation as the exemplar of everything transitory, The Getty Center stands for something very different. It stands for the Los Angeles that today has eleven universities and colleges and more than forty museums, the Los Angeles that was a second home to Arnold Schoenberg and Thomas Mann, to Frank Lloyd Wright and Richard Neutra. For this Los Angeles, The Getty Center represents stability, continuity, and a long, slow evolution of intellectual and material culture. But The Getty Center is not a monastic retreat. It is not a place where one asks, "Who am I?"

It is a place to ask, "Who are we?" This is crucial in Los Angeles, which without question is one of the most multiethnic and multilingual cities on earth. The architecture has to create an ideal version of the social space of the city itself. It has to bring people together, allowing them to mingle, but never crowding them, never forcing a meeting. The relationship of one building to another, of space to space within each building,

Ara Pacis Museum, Rome; front entrance

resulted in plans for the reorganization and upgrading of the surrounding Augustan area. The site has particularly delicate characteristics because of its outstanding historical, archaeological, and architectural values and the design for the new museum of the Ara Pacis was conceived not only as a museum dedicated to the preservation and display of a single object but also as an integral part of the larger context of the staggeringly rich urban fabric of historic Rome.

Despite the variety of scale and program among the museums featured in this volume, interrelated ideas about the basic dialogues between public and private space and between building and context emerge in each. I believe it is possible to see my work as a sequence of investigation into the spatial interchange between public and private realms.

The goal is to provide spaces for people to come together as social groups, spaces for individual contemplation and solitude, and for the flow between these two extremes. This interchange has perhaps its greatest potential for expression in the creation of the museum. The architect brings to the design of museums an ability to shape the space, to control the light, to organize the program, to create a pattern of circulation, and to creatively use and reinforce the museum's aesthetic values.

Those who use the museum should benefit from being in this particular place not only to observe and relate to the works of art, but also to experience the architecture.

I believe that the museum's purpose is to pursue cultural enlightenment, and, to my mind, this mission could also be used to inform the architectural conception. The museum can be both literally and metaphysically radiant. It can become a beacon of the cultural life of the city and of the community.

R. Meier, "Preface", in *Richard Meier: Museums: 1973-2006*, New York: Rizzoli, 2006, pp. 8-9.

Scott Frances

J. Paul Getty Center for the Fine Arts, Los Angeles 1996
pp. 94, 96-97, 98, 99

Museum of Contemporary Art, MACBA, Barcellona 1995
pp. 100-101, 102, 103, 104-105

Sandra Day Federal Courthouse, Phoenix 2000
pp. 106-107, 108-109

Photographers

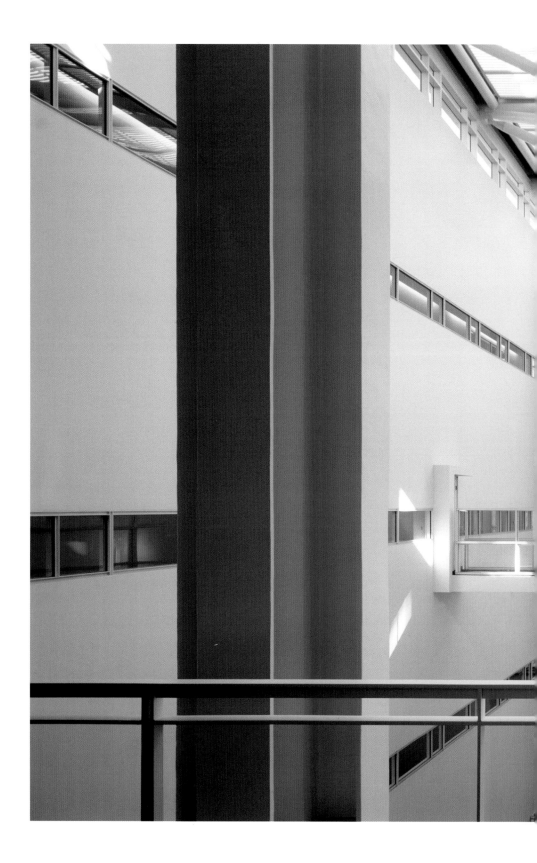

Critique

Bordering Utopia

Collin Rowe
Introduction

Which is again to establish that the *physique* and the *morale* of modern architecture, its flesh and its word, were (and could) never be coincident; and it is when we recognize that neither word nor flesh was ever coincident with itself, let alone with each other, that, without undue partiality, we can approach the present day. For under the circumstances what to do? If we believe that modern architecture did establish one of the great hopes of the world – always, in detail, ridiculous, but never, *in toto,* to be rejected – then do we adhere to *physique-flesh* or to *morale-word?*
To repeat: this choice became visible once it became almost too evident to bear that the central and socialist mission of modern architecture had failed – or, alternatively, that this mission had become dissolved in the sentimentalities and bureaucracies of the welfare state. The simple fusion of art and technology, of symbolical gesture and functional requirement was now not to be made; and, in default of this fusion, a variety of alternatives have offered themselves.
These have included what has already been listed: Miesian neoclassicism (with some kind of dependent theory of Platonic form); the New Brutalism (with the inference that self-flagellation may elicit the better world); the Futurist Revival (with the very popular supposition that science fiction might provide the ultimate hope);
and the *neo-art nouveau* (which, both in its Shingle Style and Italian ramifications, insists that if we only retreat to the Eighteen-Nineties – and also simulate a naivete – then health will inevitably ensue.
And, to this catalogue, there must al so be added the notion that we ignore the situation altogether: that, in default of that convenient anti-"art" entity of the Twenties called "the machine," we substitute the equally useful entities designated "the computer" and "the people" and that, if these two abstractions are absolutely at variance with each other, we will not indulge ourselves in too many scruples about

this problem. It is a problem which exists only in the minds of the far too sensitive; and if research and data-collection are the wave of the future – if the public wisdom so indicates – then it is certainly to the future we belong.
It is in this context of choices (none of them very agreeable) that we should place what is here published; and, having recognized this context, we should not then be too ready to impute charges of irresponsibility. It is difficult to generalize the work of these five architects. Eisenman seems to have received a revelation in Corno; Hejduk seems to wish affiliation both to Synthetic Cubist Paris and Constructivist Moscow. Nor will the more obviously Corbusian orientation of Graves, Gwathmey and Meier so readily succumb to all encompassing observations. But, for all this, there is a point of view shared which is quite simply this: that, rather than constantly to endorse the revolutionary myth, it might be more reasonable and more modest to recognize that, in the opening years of this century, great revolutions in thought occurred and that then profound visual discoveries resulted, that these are still unexplained, and that rather than assume intrinsic change to be the prerogative of every generation, it might be more useful to recognize that certain changes are so enormous as to impose a directive which cannot be resolved in any individual life span.
Or, at least, such would seem to be the argument. It concerns the plastic and spatial inventions of Cubism and the proposition that, whatever may be said about these, they possess an eloquence and a flexibility which continues now to be as overwhelming as it was then. It is an argument largely about the physique of building and only indirectly about its morale; but, since it should also be envisaged as some sort of interrogation of the mid-twentieth century architect's capacity to indulge his mostly trivial moral enthusiasm at the expense of any physical product, it might also be appropriate to conclude what has been a largely negative introduction – an attack upon a potential attack – with a series of related questions which might, ambiguously, help to establish the *meaning* – if any – in Aldo Van Eyck's terms, of what is here

presented. Is it necessary that architecture should be simply a logical derivative from functional and technological facts; and, indeed, can it ever be this?

Is it necessary that a series of buildings should imply a vision of a new and better world; and, if this is so (or even if it is not) then how frequently can a significant vision of a new and better world be propounded?

Is the architect simply a victim of circumstances? And should he be? Or may he be allowed to cultivate his own free will? And are not culture and civilization the products of the imposition of will? What is the *zeitgeist;* and, if this is a critical fiction, may the . architect act contrariwise to its alleged dictates?

How permissible is it to make use of precedent; and therefore, how legitimate is the argument that the repetition of a form is a destruction of authenticity?

Can an architecture which professes an objective of continuous experiment ever become congruous with the idea of an architecture which is to be popular, intelligible, and profound?

C. Rowe, "Introduction", in *Five Architects. Eisenman Graves Gwathmey Hejduk Meier*, New York: Oxford University Press, 1975, p. 7. With permission of Oxford University Press, Inc.

Manfredo Tafuri
Richard Meier: the mechanics of function

The work of Richard Meier – even more than that of Gwathmey & Siegel – deviates from the linguistic absolutism so characteristic of Hejduk, Eisenman and Graves. It is no mere coincidence, in fact, that in the 1972 book dedicated to the "Five," Meier is represented only by Smith House (1965) and Saltzman House (1967). Both these homes, built in a layered structure, reflect the relationship between consistence in volume and effects of transparency. An analysis of the possible geometric connections permits the formulation of analogies with the syntactic purism of Eisenman and even the ambiguous metaphors of Graves. It is indeed

undeniable that the two houses evoke an ambience of "enchantment," given their absolute detachment from their context. Further, they also manifest a trace of irony, as in the contrast between the immateriality of the glazed box and the materiality of the chimney or crown in Smith House, for example. Yet there appears to be a reminiscence of Loos, famed architect of the Tzara home, in the Saltzman House, in which the window allows a view into the interior, as though challenging the ambiguous geometry of the prism with the rounded apex, built along a diagonal matrix.

Saltzman House certainly falls within the realms of the "suspended tonality" evident in Whig Hall or Bye House or, better still, Weinstein House in Old Westbury (1971). Here, the insistence on length is evocative of the purist, metaphysical distillations of Figini & Pollini, Dujker or Howe & Lescaze in the 1930s. In Weinstein House, nonetheless, the long ramp connecting the rare residential structures is visible inside the glazed gallery with its semi-circular roof. This is redolent of the architecture typical of Victorian conservatories, albeit indirect reference to the re-interpretations of James Stirling. This harsh interruption of the elementary chain of structures introduces an ironic note. In the upper portion of the house, thin steel pillars are bared to lend support to the suspended corner on the upper floor, revealing the curvilinear block built into the lower cavity.

In a recent presentation of his own designs, Richard Meier, in breaking down his design instruments, emphasised the importance of circulation, inside and outside the buildings. Graves and Hejduk also emphasise the "passageway" element. Horizontal and vertical passageways had a precise role in the small-scale architecture of Le Corbusier – that of reproducing, inside every individual architectural object, the free relationship between road and buildings postulated for urban scale operations. Meier does not follow Le Corbusier's symbolism or Hejduk's abstractionism. Formations for passageways, as well as clarity of the organisational system, supporting structures and entrances are, in his view, just design materials to be put together to form a whole after they have been individually researched. The complexity of joining them makes the architectural result irrefutable. Invention is the pillar stone upon which the dimension of function finds a base.

In any debate aimed at proving that architecture is the mark of pure structure, Eisenman is the best source of support. In America, in any case, his work is the best testimonial to such a belief. If, instead, architecture is deemed to be a "system of systems," involving various overlapping yet distinct foundations, then Meier would provide the best examples. The comparison between two projects apparently centred on a single theme will serve to illustrate: Eisenman's House 111 and Meier's David Hoffmarm House. In the former, two solids rotating around each other silently display the result of the arbitrary act that has put them in place. In the latter, it is the connection between forms that counts, their combination. Distant models seem to be the Kallenbach House of Gropius and Adolf Meyer (1921) as well as some expressionist designs by the Luckhardt brothers and Fritz Kaldenbach. In other words, Meier proposes a design inspection method that relies on free variation in which the initial isolation of the components, paired with the verification of a coded typology, does not obstruct the subsequent combination task. Within this retrieval of the "sign function" – and here the term function is given its widest meaning – Meier can afford tacit criticism of the conceptualistic reduction of the sign-structure relationship operated by Eisenman. No more merciless chaining of geometry to its incredible stillness or studies of "deep structures" and no more attempts, as in Graves, to extract multi-meaningful messages from the signs. Meier's geometry also excludes attempts at semantic recovery; the division of the signs testifies to the presence of objects which display their function, with absolute proof.

Rykwert wrote that "Meier's architecture is always understated and yet always assertive through its insistently complex geometry, which he somehow always reduces to appearing absolutely inevitable. That is his strength, the assertion of an inevitable order, which exalts the functional pattern of the occupation. Meier is a maker of objects whose power lies in the obsessive elegance of their cut, in their cool though exemplary and somehow didactic detachment from their surroundings."

This is evident in projects such as that of Pound Ridge, where the themes of Smith House and Saltzman House overlap, achieving poetry in the "dynamic balance" that even historical models could find something to envy. In this case, it might perhaps be more exact to speak of "nostalgia," however. It is a classic example of survival, not revival. Rykwert's judgment might still hold pertinence for the four designs created by Meier for the American Division of the Olivetti Corporation, or for the prototypes of flexible, industrial buildings (sic!). Such designs demonstrate, among other things, the unbiased experimentalism of Meier's research typology (see the use of the serpentine plans in the Olivetti Residence of 1973 in Tarrytown, where the hinging of the end blocks, the concentration of toilet blocks and the vertical connection along with the treatment of the surfaces allude to a kind of criticism toward the Alver Aalto model of the MIT dormitories at Cambridge).

This part of Meier's research, however, may well be incomprehensible without an understanding of the relationship he developed between experimental research and large-scale design. Such relationship was already evident in the Physical Health Education Facility for the State University College of Fredonia (1972) and the Bronx School in New York (1973-1975). As Meier himself points out, the extension of the stairway in the Fredonia complex is in line with the same organisational principles of Smith House and Saltzman House. The various nuclei are included on a backbone that animates them and gives them form. Here it is possible to criticise the again laborious formation of the large circular space of I. Pei with the tangentially juxtaposed building. In the Bronx School, however, an assembly of residential equipment for 750 mentally challenged children and the positioning of the units around a central space reflect a return to a typically urban dimension of the public-private space relationship. In other words, Meier seems to have adopted a deeply critical process, returning to certain stages already employed by the classical "masters" of the modern movement. This is

exemplified by the use of richly metaphoric objects, technological valuables and a perfect form within an urban context.

In a project like Douglas House in Michigan Beach (1973), Meier furthered the studies begun with Saltzman House and the house at Pound Ridge, where his expression found meaning in solutions that favoured "opposition," in a style oscillating between transparency (the front) and full and partial surfaces (the back). In Saltzman House, however, the constituent "mechanism" is accentuated. Though the outline of the structure is vaguely reminiscent of Stirling and the "Machine Age," what is most important in this project is that the object attaches itself ostentatiously to the environment, rising up from the external stairway. The two stairways and the long suspended walkway, which leads from the hills behind the house to the upper terrace, form an independent system of walkways, joining to the house via the

long corridor and hallways. Douglas House thus imposed an exchange between autonomous objects and external space. This should perhaps be understood as the premise for Meier's urban housing designs.

In association with Emery Roth & Sons, Meier & Associates developed a residential complex for Madison Ass. and Tishman Realty and Construction Corporation in the middle of Manhattan. The final project houses 600 residential units and 300,000 sq.m reserved as office space. A unique, rectangular mono block, centred round a green area – reminiscent of Le Corbusier – leads to a combination of irregular geometric blocks. A single building stands tall, connected to a terraced structure joining a second complex, it too characterised by terracing and ascension. Again research was laborious and did not lend itself well to a general model. Even Meier blocked his own research to the limits of Utopia; projected directly

Western façade of the Hoffman House (1966-1967) with extroverted chimney and hood

115

Western façade
of the Douglas House
(1971-1973) with its
large windows overlooking
Lake Michigan

with that of Giovanni Pasanella's for Twin Parks Southwest, a manneristic renovation of the Unité di Marsiglia in which the relationship between private and public space remains undefined. Meier's alternative proposal swings between acceptance of the existing urban network and its deformation, in accordance with a precise definition of socially usable spaces. Frampton writes: "One may argue that the overall parts of the Meier scheme stem from a curious compound of Le Corbusier (after Henard) on the one hand, and Sittesque notions of urban space on the other. The unusual formal and social interaction that the Meier scheme invokes in conjunction with the existing urban context no doubt derives from this conscious attempt to conflate two ultimately antithetical models taken from 19th-century urban theory."

The building projection renders the rest an explicit apparition in one of Meier's preliminary designs for Twin Parks. In the construction however, the plan crumbled and was altered, respecting or altering the existing alignments, finally joining with the two high blocks at the opposite ends of the plan. That which has been referred to as Meier's "realism," finds its utmost accomplishment in Twin Parks. Henard's and Corbu's plan has been criticised for its claim to have attained a universal solution for "bad" urban areas. Yet there is not even a drop of nostalgia for that model. Rather, it is associated with detachment, criticised and described as having fallen into a contradictory reality, like that of the Bronx slums. Such relegation seems to want to emphasise the limitations of the operation itself, of its being a social service, which is nonetheless powerless compared to the complexity of metropolitan conflicts. (Twin Parks was to expand and it would not have solved those conflicts.) This explains Meier's linguistic rejection on this occasion. The rigorous conciseness of the spaces is in line with the rejection of typological invention; no satisfied neo-brutalism of the material, but a subtle cadence of rhythmic tedium, in which minimal variations serve to accentuate the compactness of the brick body, its desperate unity. Hence, assonance with the existing building has deep significance. Here too, no populism. The refinement of the cuts at the edge of the surfaces

onto urban scale, the continuity of the walkways is again introduced as "Ariadne's thread," providing directional assistance with the maze of passageways. This "direction" is neither unique nor definitive, however, nor does it solve or propose to cancel the problem or the contradiction of the operation. It also does not create a non chaotic organization.

One might speak of a profound "critical realism" when discussing Meier's urban projects. Fine examples are FHA's exceptional renovation of the Westbeth – the first of New York City's special zoning districts – and the estate at Twin Parks Northeast, created for the UDC.

Kenneth Frampton rightly compares Meier's solution

and the geometrical deformations of the end blocks exclude any sentimentality; the linguistic reduction has at its foundation an ulterior model: the "less is more" motto of Mies. More specifically, this is the Mies of the residential blocks in Berlin's Afrikanische Strasse (1925) more than the American Mies. This, then, is architecture at two levels; the first, all socially usable, the second, reserved for those who know how to read the profound meanings of the rejection of reloading the forms of impossible myths.

The small-scale analysis of works carried out between 1965 and1970 thus has a final destination; it was one of the best residential studies of present-day America. Experimentation regarding the possible autonomy of an architectural expression-function painfully concludes (temporarily) with a reflection of the limits of the language itself and the proposed abilities of an invented typology.

In Meier's last design projects – the Museum of Modern Art in Villa Strozzi, Florence (1973), and the student residences at Cornell University (1974) – invention tends toward an exasperated inspection of the architectural imagination. It is difficult, however, to recognise where the reserve of the form finishes, and where an ancestral, puritan anguish starts.

M. Tafuri, "Richard Meier: la meccanica delle funzioni", from "Les bijoux indiscrets", in *Five architects. NY*, catalogue for the exhibit in Naples, edited by C. Gubitosi and A. Izzo, Rome: Officina Edizioni, 1976, pp. 24-28.

Werner Blaser
Architectural Principles for a New Aesthetic in the Work of Richard Meier

Architectural principles can be characterized per se solely by equilibrium, unity and their power to command attention.

Richard Meier has an unquestioning love of beauty, animated by a creative spirit of great significance. He never wearies of analysing the opportunities a museum building affords the architect, and this constitutes an unfailing source of cultural and intellectual inspiration for his work. What is of supreme importance here is his treatment of the structure in a dialogue with the site, not merely in the sense of adaptation to existing features but also a s a principle for a new aesthetic. Although the reference is to a different context, the catalogue on the architect Emil Steffan may be appositely quoted in this connection: "The challenge to the architect – and his reward – does not reside simply in meeting the demands of existing sites and a landscape but rather in establishing within one corner of the world a new "place" – a genius loci – by his ordering and creative sense."

Richard Meier's concept is based on the idea of making his buildings consistently white in appearance. The restraint evoked by white creates a timeless elegance and grace, especially in a museum. Such an open-minded attitude is reflected in the building. Interiors are thus created that are memorable for their sensitive handling: light and dark, enclosed and open, functional and meditative. Connoisseurs and patrons of art admire the skill with which interdisciplinary exhibition rooms are correlated in an entirely natural manner with window-wall access ways leading to recreation areas. These groups of rooms are marked by lightness, clarity and a precise identity. The light zone is surrounded by darkness. A feeling of confinement (concentration) and expanse (contemplation) is induced. The radiant white makes the room not only luminous also more spacious, mysterious and, one might almost say, festive in spirit.

The Norwegian architect and architectural critic Christian Norberg-Schulz, reminds us of what architecture is called upon to do; namely, to create identifiable places, to interpret space and the world we live in not with metaphorical tricks but by exploiting their most basic resources: opening and enclosure, load and load-bearing, concentration and expansion, economy and extravagance. The past must, he says, serve the present and lead us back to former principles which we have to reinterpret with the means and materials of today.

That is why good architecture is invariably based on principles – but shuns modes and trends. Unless he is content to copy existing models without thinking, every building designer will turn primarily to the logic of objective laws to find qualities; buildings of high merit are unique – we identify ourselves with them. The basic elements of the design, the technical necessities, and the question of materials are all factors that are directly responsible for giving the building its precise character. One of the outstanding features of Richard Meier's work is the scale that values simplicity and elemental things and marks out the rooms he elaborates as places to be experienced by all who come to enjoy the art displayed there. Art moves and has its being in the triangle between studio, gallery and museum, with the museum serving as a repository where what has proved to be of lasting worth can be exhibited. The museum is built for permanence; the object of art may be subject to constant change. This is why there can be no equivalence between building and art, only reciprocal stimulation. Good architecture has always been used for a multitude of purposes. An open plan makes for freedom in combination and variation. It is this ability to adapt the interior to other needs as they arise that makes the excellence of good architecture. The building derives its form from what the interior is actually called upon to express.

In the following we shall endeavor to see the Vitruvian principles of architecture and their significance for the present in relation to the examples of Richard Meier. We are therefore essentially concerned with a confrontation with works in which the embodiment of Vitruvian principles is most clearly expressed. This continual confrontation calls for sophisticated thought which is invariably critical of itself and refuses to tolerate a merely accidental form, fashionable though such

a concession may be in appearance. In Richard Meier's work there are no academic demonstrations of theories and speculations. For building is synonymous with function, and architecture synonymous with art.

Vitruvius's principles of architecture were rediscovered in the universities and academies of the 20th century and have been extended by the addition of the following maxims: fitness for purpose solves the whole design problem; construction is the static process in building; space is enclosure and opening; proportion is scale in harmony; material is unity in texture; art is the symbolic element in a building. The architect seeks to bring the content of his commission into a shape as a building. The content relates to the technical and practical function. Form is the expression of the interplay between aesthetics and intellect. The building must therefore have an instrumental quality while at the same time manifesting an unmistakable form. To this extent use and form determine the building.

Ever since the ancient Roman engineer and architectural theorist Vitruvius (1st century BC) formulated the basic principles of architecture (*De architectura, Ten Books on Architecture,* published in Rome, 1484), permanence and monumentality have been demanded in building. To stimulate thought, we will take a look at the way in which Vitruvius classified the criteria or aspects of architecture – a classification which, curiously enough, is still applicable today. He taught appropriateness and usefulness (utilitas), strength and durability (firmitas) and beauty or amenity (venustas).

W. Blaser, "Architectural Principles for a New Aesthetic in the Work of Richard Meier" in R. Meier, *Building for Art / Bauen für die Kunst,* edited by W. Blaser, Basel-Boston-Berlin: Birkhäuser Verlag, 1990.

Bibliography

R. Meier, *Richard Meier architect: buildings and projects 1966-76*, New York: Oxford University Press, 1976.

R. Meier, *Building the Getty*, A.A. Knopf, New York: 1997.

Five Architects: Eisenman Graves Gwathmey Hejduk Meier, edited by George Wittenborn & Company, New York: 1972.

Five Architects NY, catalogue for the exhibit in Naples, edited by C. Gubitosi and A. Izzo, Rome: Officina Edizioni, 1976.

M. Tafuri, "Le ceneri di Jefferson", in *La sfera e il labirinto Avanguardie e architettura da Piranesi agli anni '70*, Turin: Einaudi, 1980, pp. 361-371.

Richard Meier: Architectures: 1964-1984, New York: Rizzoli, 1984.

Richard Meier. Building for Art Bauen für die Kunst, edited by W. Blaser, Basel-Boston-Berlin: Birkhäuser Verlag, 1990.

Richard Meier Buildings and Projects 1979-1989, London: Academy Editions, 1990.

Richard Meier / Frank Stella. Arte e architettura, edited by M. Costanzo, V. Giorgi, M.G. Tolomeo, catalogue for the exhibit in Rome, Milan: Electa, 1993.

Richard Meier, edited by P. Corra, Milan: Electa, 1993.

Richard Meier, architect, 1992-1999, New York: Rizzoli, 1999.

K. Frampton, "ad vocem Richard Alan Meier" in *Dizionario dell'Architettura del XX Secolo*, edited by C. Olmo, IV, Turin: Umberto Allemandi & C., 2001, pp. 264-269.

Richard Meier, edited by K. Frampton, Milan: Electa, 2003.

A. Falzetti, *La chiesa di Dio Padre misericordioso di Richard Meier*, Rome: CLEAR, 2003.

Richard Meier: Museums: 1973-2006, New York: Rizzoli, 2006.

Richard Meier. Il museo dell'Ara Pacis, Milan: Electa, 2007.

Photographic references

Claudia Conforti, Rome: 76 top
© dbox, New York: 78, 80, 81, 85
© Christopher Felver / Corbis: 86
© Scott Frances / Esto: 14-15, 22, 44, 51, 52, 53,
55, 56, 57, 59, 60, 61, 64, 71, 72, 73 bottom, 91, 92,
100-101, 102, 103, 104-105, 106-107, 108-109
Scott Frances / Esto © The J. Paul Getty Trust:
cover, 10-11, 12-13, 46, 48, 49, 91, 94,
96-97, 98, 99
Andrea Jemolo, Rome: 6, 24, 25, 66-69
© Alan Karchmer / Esto: 8-9, 63, 65
© Mark Seliger, New York: 18, 28, rear cover
Ezra Stoller © Esto: 16-17, 20, 23, 26, 32, 34, 36, 37,
39, 40, 41, 42, 45, 110, 115, 116
© Edmund Sumner / View / Esto: 93
© Albert Vecerka / Esto: 73 top
© www.scottfrances.com: 74, 75, 76-77, 77 bottom

For all pictures and sketches, unless otherwise
indicated, © Richard Meier & Partners Architects LLP,
New York.

The authors would like to thank: the architect
Richard Meier for the kindness and time afforded us;
Mary Lou Bunn and Laura Galvanek from the Meier
studio in New York for their helpfulness and pleasant
manner with which they welcomed us and introduced
us to the studio's work, and the painter Mila Dau
for the generous hospitality.

The publisher is available for any queries regarding
pictures that have not been accredited.